M000028036

PURSUIT
of a
Thirsty
Fool

Pursuit of a Thirsty Fool
Copyright © 2011 T.J. MacLeslie

Published by
BottomLine Media
a ministry of Pioneers-USA
10123 William Carey Dr.
Orlando
FL 32832

All rights reserved. No part of this publication may be reproduced in any form by any means, electronic, mechanical, photocopy, recording or otherwise, without the prior permission of the publisher, except as provided for by USA copyright law.

Cover and page design by Neil Angove Ltd (*neilangove.ltd.uk*) and Eric Powell Design
Cover photo by Matthew Cook (*biscuitpictures.co.uk*)

First printing, 2011

All scripture quotations are taken from the Holy Bible,
New International Version®, NIV®.
Copyright ©1973, 1978, 1984 by Biblica, Inc.™
Used by permission of Zondervan.
All rights reserved worldwide. *www.zondervan.com*

Trade paperback ISBN: 978-0-9759997-4-5

BottomLine Media celebrates the bottom line of God's covenant with Abraham:
"I will bless all nations through you."

For more information on Pioneers, visit *pioneers.org*

CONTENTS

ENDORSEMENTS

In telling the story of his life, T.J. MacLeslie challenges many of the sacred cows and long-held beliefs of evangelicals. This book is a must read for all who have struggled with life, with faith, with the question of the reality of God.
David L. Wickstrom, Ph.D.
clinical psychologist and missions consultant

God has used T.J. MacLeslie to turn my focus ever more to pursuing the relationship with the Father for which I was made. God is the unabashed hero of this book, and T.J. MacLeslie a servant He is using to bring glory to His name.
Matthew VanderHeiden
Academic Dean and Lecturer in Hermeneutics
and Expository Preaching, Portuguese Bible Institute

This book is an insightful travelogue of a God-ordained journey. Anyone who reads it will be challenged to acknowledge that God never gives up on us.
a missionary in East Asia

Reading Pursuit accomplishes what good pastoring always does: it opens the eyes of your heart so that you can see your life as a story and God as the story's unseen Author.
a missionary in China

There is a fine line between detailing the sordid mess of our lives and highlighting the beauty of God's grace. In my opinion T.J. MacLeslie gets this right.
Graham Phillimore
a retired minister

If you have ever felt you are beyond redemption, this is the book for you. Clearly, this journey is a struggle limited not only to one wayward life, but to myriad others all over Christendom.

JFK Mensah
missions leader

T.J. MacLeslie gives us a tremendous gift: a bare knuckles telling of his brokenness, a crystal clear view into the most intimate places of his soul and a transparent rendering of his life's journey of discovering intimacy with God.

Jim Roden
lead pastor, The Journey Evangelical Free Church, Tucson, Arizona

I have known the author since he was in grade school, and reconnected with him again through reading *Pursuit*. I could not put the book down!

Jim Fredericks
former pastor and missionary

PREFACE

Writing this book has been a very personal journey, but not a lonely one. They say it takes a village to raise a child; it certainly took a community to create this book.

Throughout the process, I have felt propelled along by the Spirit of God, encouraged by the Father and reassured by the Son. I do not know what He will do with it, but I know I was supposed to write it. I knew He was calling me to write, but I didn't know what. So, I sat down and started writing. As the thoughts became sentences and the sentences paragraphs, this book began to take shape.

The writing was hard, but the editing was even more difficult for me. It was tough to receive the honest critiques of friends, but because of their input, the book you are holding is better than the one that spilled from my fingertips. I want to thank each of my friends and family who inflicted the "wounds of a friend" to make this book what it is today. I could not have done this without you.

Some of you I have been close to for years. You have spoken into my life and shaped me by your words as well as your lives. Others of you were acquaintances at the beginning of this process but have become friends in the midst of it. All of you have mentored me in this, and I am grateful for each of you.

I would especially like to thank my wife who has endured much as I have worked through this writing process. You have had to put up with a grumpy man as I have delved into the painful past. It was a learning curve for both of us, and I am grateful for your unwavering support throughout. I love you.

I also want to thank my children. Although you have not yet read this, you have lived through the process of its creation. I pray that you will avoid my mistakes, even as I am sure you will make mistakes of your own. I love you. I loved you before you were born, and I will always love you. No matter what you do, where you go or who you become, I will always be your father, and you will always be my beloved children.

Wales, 2010

A RUDE AWAKENING

The sound of ringing disturbs my dream. As I grudgingly return to consciousness, I realize that the source of the sound is not in my dream, but is in the waking world.

There's a phone ringing in the room. But, I don't have a phone in my room! Where am I?

As I slowly drag myself from slumber to wakefulness, I hear a woman's voice answering the phone.

Who is she?

I roll over and realize where I am, who she is and what I have done. In that moment, she hands me the phone with the words, "It is for you."

I take the phone from her hands, trying hard to avoid her quizzical gaze. My voice is still heavy with sleep as I mumble, "Hello, who is this?"

I am jolted back to reality by my mother's voice on the other end of the line. She asks who answered the phone. My fuzzy mind reaches for a convenient lie to cut her short, and I discover the reason for the call. She explains that I need to fly home to America because I have been selected to spend a year as a missionary.

My mind whips back and forth between these two opposing truths. I have just been chosen to tell people about the good news that God is real, He loves them and He wants to have a relationship with them. I have also just spent the night in bed with a woman I hardly even know. I cannot immediately reconcile these wildly different worlds. I tell my mom that I'll call her back, hang up quickly and turn over to face yet more questions.

This rude awakening was not just a call from my mother. This was a divine ambush, an intervention by the Father of all, reaching out yet again to one of His children. At my lowest point, He awoke me from my slumber with a ringing phone. It was at this most shameful and debased moment in my life that God called me to Himself. I am so very grateful that He did.

As I reflect back on my life, I can see that God has been pursuing me the whole time. He has always been there, behind the smiles of strangers or in the longing I feel as I wonder at the sky aflame with a brilliant sunset. He has been wooing me from before time. He laid foundations in my life and set blessings in motion from before I was born. He has been loving me and protecting me throughout my journey. He has been persistently pursuing, and I have resisted His advances. Like the patient lover that He is, He has allowed me to wander, scattering messages of love and hope along the road, reminding me of His presence and His love. He beckons me to come to Him.

I have nothing but respect and admiration for those who hear His call and immediately turn. They seem to instantly recognize that He is the answer to their search. There are those whose road is direct, whose way is straight. Mine has been the journey of a prodigal pilgrim. My journey has been a searching, a wandering down twisted roads with many detours. Many of my detours and trials were self-inflicted; some were the results of others' choices and actions. From my current vantage point, I see the ways that He has redeemed even these dark and painful experiences. He has brought light from the darkness and produced healing through wounds.

All along the way, God has continued to insert Himself into my life and into my heart. He has consistently intervened and interrupted. He has drawn me to Himself. I am desperate for God. I crave Him, I need Him and I want Him. I get glimpses of Him, have experiences with Him and they always leave me strangely filled yet longing for more. My life feels like an odd sort of stumbling forward.

I am a thirsty fool. I am thirsty for Him, but am foolish enough to wander off the path that leads me to Him. My experience hasn't been one of steady ascent, but an Exodus-like journey full of revelation and rebellion, manna and snakes. But like the Israelites of old, God has been constantly present and has been guiding me, even in my detours, to accomplish His good plans for my life. I am so glad I've finally found the sweet submission that has led me into a life lived with Him.

My prayer is that others might find hope as they read an honest account of my journey. That others who, like me, haven't found the road to God a straight one, might be encouraged to seek again. That reading about my longings, my failures and my victories might cause some to dare to long again. I hope as you read this story you will be inspired and encouraged to embark upon or continue on your own journey towards Him.

CHAPTER 1

FOUNDATIONS

In some ways, my story has a rather conventional beginning. I was raised in a Christian home. My parents loved the Lord and loved us kids as well as they knew how—which was pretty well, all things considered. We had dinner together nearly every night. We played games and sang songs together. We went fishing and camping. In a thousand ways, some verbal some not, they told us they loved us. I never questioned, and never do question, my parents' love for me. They made me know that I was lovable. This is perhaps the most amazing gift I ever received from them.

Our church was like a second home to us. I can't remember a time we didn't go regularly. Growing up, I felt like we were there whenever the doors to the church were open. The conservative evangelical church we attended preached the Bible faithfully. I am grateful to have been raised around such staunch people of faith. They tried hard to understand the Bible and apply it to their lives.

It was because of these dear people that I began to read the Bible as a child and to commit some of it to memory. Of course, I understood very little of what I memorized, and my reasons for doing so sprung from my competitive nature and a desire for the candy that our teachers handed out as rewards. They encouraged us to invite Jesus "into our hearts" and to receive forgiveness. It wasn't until many years later that the seeds of truth sown in my youth would take root and God would use these long dormant seeds to bear fruit in my life.

I loved the church where we grew up. The people were kind and generous, and the potluck dinners were delicious. Our family was one of the pillars of the church, and we kids were surrounded by a world of caring adults. There were picnics, barbecues and a host of fun activities for us, but there were other currents swirling. Darker things, of which I was blissfully unaware as a child, lurked beneath the surface.

I had a lot of questions. Even as a child I was curious about not just the *whats* of life but the *hows* and the *whys*. I was always trying to make sense of the world around me. I soon found that my questions weren't welcomed, but rather unwanted and even threatening. I didn't know it at the time, but I was running smack into the fear of questions. Questions meant doubt, and doubt was bad. Certainty was equated with faith, and doubt was the opposite of faith. We were taught that we shouldn't doubt but instead believe. I wish I had a nickel for every time I heard the phrase, "The Bible says it. I believe it. That settles it!" Perhaps that kind of faith comes easily for some, but it certainly did not for me.

As I look back, I have to wonder how the leaders of that conservative evangelical church could have studied the Scriptures so much and still presented such a distorted picture of God. I now realize that much of what we believe about life, the universe and God is a result of our culture rather than a true picture of what is real. We tend to simply repeat what we've been taught. We don't naturally question what we have received from those we trust and respect. As a child, I was taught very clearly about who God is and was assured that this is the correct and "biblical" picture of God.

I was taught that God had three distinct parts or persons within Him: the Father, the Son and the Holy Spirit. They were each equally God but possessed different roles. God the Father is the King of the Universe, the Judge, the Ruler. Jesus died to save us from the wrath of God. The Holy Spirit inspired the writing of Scripture. These are partial truths, but in teaching these partial truths, we have distorted the whole. We have created a God who fits well within our systems and our culture. In doing so, we have done violence to Scripture and have presented a twisted picture of the nature and character of God.

Along the road of life and in the pages of Scripture, I have found a fuller picture of God. Not an entirely different picture, but a more accurate one. One that is real and compelling. I have found another Father, another Jesus and another Holy Spirit as well. I still know the Father to be the Creator and King of the Universe, but not a harsh tyrant hell-bent on judgment. I have met Him as a Father longing to be known and to reveal Himself. I have met Jesus, not only as the sacrificial lamb to save us from the wrath of the Father, but as a brother and a friend. He has shown me how to live in step with the loving and ever-present Father. Jesus has removed the barriers so that I can enter into the presence of the Father and boldly approach His throne with the confidence of one dearly loved. I have discovered the Holy Spirit to be alive and active. I have heard His voice. He guides and directs, comforts and speaks, with a gentle strength that is sweetness to my soul.

These three live in perfect harmony and community. They are always at work. They invite us into their family to enjoy their presence and to partner in their work. All three have become real to me along the way.

This relational, communal, intimate and inviting God is actually the God revealed in the Scriptures. The God who longs to meet us along the way. But, I didn't know any of this as a child.

As I grew up, questions began to push their way to the surface of my mind. Our church talked about God the Father all the time, and Jesus was an ever-present part of our services, but the Holy Spirit almost never came up. I asked about this at some point and was warned against leaning on experience. I was even told a cautionary tale about a man who had wanted more and had gone off the deep end and become a "charismatic." I didn't know what that meant, but I could tell from the disapproving looks and shaking heads that this must have been a terrible fate indeed. When I expressed my desire to know God and to hear from God more personally, I was firmly reprimanded.

A man I respected asked me, "What makes you so special that God would want to speak to you directly? Who do you think you are?" He went on to say, "God has given us the Bible. If you want to hear His voice, you should read it! That is how God speaks to us today. Everything else is just emotion and trickery, or even a deception from the devil himself!"

That didn't sound quite right to me. After all, I had been taught time and time again, "Christianity is a relationship not a religion." I had been told, "Jesus is your friend," and that prayer is "talking to Jesus." It didn't sound right to me that, while I could speak to God, God couldn't speak to me.

The people in my church loved and worshiped the Almighty God, but they also taught that He no longer spoke and no longer intervened in the world. I found in the pages of Scripture an active, miracle-working God, but I was told that He'd stopped that kind of thing centuries ago.

My father was a leader in the church, and one day I asked him about this apparent contradiction. He encouraged my thirst for God and assured me that I shouldn't worry too much about what our church taught in this particular area. He encouraged me instead to read and study the Scriptures. He cautioned me against leaning too much on subjective experience but also warned me not to put God in a box. He taught me to respect my elders but also to not believe something merely because someone in a position of authority had said it. He encouraged me to use my mind and to investigate everything for myself. This was another gift my parents gave me.

My parents gave me many wonderful gifts, but there were other legacies they passed on I would rather not have inherited. From my mother I received the fear of man. I can still hear her concerned tone as she asked, "What will people think?" Many times my siblings and I would start squabbling on the way to church in the back seat of the family Oldsmobile. My mother would try to silence us by asking, "What if people saw us?" I was puzzled by her questions as a young child, but at some point, I stopped questioning the questions. I began to internalize the fear and learned to put up a façade, to play my expected role, to make the right impression.

From my father I received the mantle of a "red-blooded American man." The picture of American manliness he painted for me was one of strength and independence. What boy doesn't aspire to live up to the image of manliness that his father praises? However, there were some dark realities behind those words. Being a "red-blooded American man" meant that anger was OK. Anger could be a powerful tool or even a useful weapon. Anger was helpful, weakness was anathema, patriotism was good and John Wayne was almost the fourth member of the Trinity. Being a "red-blooded American man" also meant that it was only natural I would want to look at, and to lust after, women.

I found the *Playboy* magazines my father kept hidden in his sock drawer. I learned, not from his words but from his actions, that pornography was OK because God made women beautiful. We were supposed to look at them. I remember my heart beating faster and the confusing mixture of shame, guilt and strange stirrings in my body when, as a child, I gazed at the images in those magazines. I soon began to act on these complicated feelings by myself. Thus began a pattern of feeling, feeding and acting on sexual urges that led to years of struggle.

My father also left me a deficit of respect. I realize now that I have spent considerable time and energy in my life looking for the respect I didn't receive from him. My father could be very expressive and loving. He also had a quick temper, which often found expression in name calling, biting sarcasm and even outright mocking. I am sure he had no idea of the damage he was doing, but, even so, the verbal blows left scars.

These few undesirable "gifts" notwithstanding, I lived a fairly sheltered existence. I loved my family, and they loved me. I loved the church and trusted those in authority. With few exceptions, my early childhood experiences were good, and the world seemed to be a bright and safe place in which to live. My life was pretty idyllic, but things took a darker turn as I approached my teenage years.

As I was growing up, I was often singled out for leadership roles—in the classroom, in sports and at church, I often heard the word "potential." "He has so much potential!" they would say. People kept telling me that I was a "natural leader." I think they meant to encourage me with words like these, but more often than not, they came with additional cautionary advice or even rebuke. "You are a natural leader, and that is why you shouldn't…" "You must be more careful in what you do, because others will follow your example."

As a child, I railed against these accolades. "I don't want anyone to follow me!" "I just want to do whatever I want to do!" "I didn't ask them to follow me!" "I didn't ask for potential or to be a natural leader!" My father's reply to my childish rants was to say, "Ask for it or not, it's what you've got. You're going to have to live with it." That sounded like a curse to my young ears!

I was encouraged to run for class president and student council. It was not uncommon for me to be selected as the team captain at recess or in organized sports. I was chosen to participate in leadership development programs both at school and at church. I suppose it was because I was singled out by adults so often that it didn't seem strange when Keith, one of the youth leaders at our church, started paying attention to me.

It was the summer before I started junior high. We had been encouraged to start attending the youth group instead of Sunday school so that we'd be ready for the coming transition in the fall. Keith was a youth staff member, probably not much older than eighteen or twenty at the time. He drove a silver sports car, and I was excited when he offered to let me steer the car as we drove home from youth meetings. He made me promise not to tell my parents. It was the first of the secrets.

Sometimes after youth events, Keith would take several of us boys out for ice cream or to a video arcade. Sometimes we would play racquetball at a gym. It was fun to be out with the guys. It made me feel more independent and grown-up. In the midst of these other activities, I didn't think twice when Keith invited some of us to a sleepover at his house. We went to see a movie first and then returned to Keith's house to sleep. I couldn't have imagined what he had in mind for that night.

It started with locker room humor. Then Keith started telling us lurid stories about women. He encouraged us to strip down to our underwear to sleep because it was "just us boys." None of it struck me as particularly wrong, but on the other hand, things didn't feel quite right either. The stories he told left me feeling aroused, confused and ashamed. Wasn't he a church youth leader? At church he talked to us about Jesus, but here in his house he was telling dirty stories.

The next time I had a sleepover at Keith's house, I was the only boy who showed up. I had expected my friends to be there, but Keith offered some excuse as to why they couldn't make it. Things went downhill quickly. He began to talk about sex and guided our conversation into ever more shocking and graphic territory.

Then it happened. I remember the demands. I remember the confusion. I remember resisting as much as a little boy knows how. I remember the shame. I remember the guilt. I remember feeling like it was my fault. I remember his nervous questions and thinly-veiled threats the next morning. I remember wondering why it had happened to me. I wondered if I should tell someone, but I was so scared and ashamed that I told no one.

A few weeks later Keith tried the same tricks with an older boy who not only resisted his advances but also told someone what had happened. The church halls rang with angry words and hateful voices. Words like homosexual, gay, faggot and queer. My father used words like these only when he was very angry, so I decided the best course of action was to keep my head down and hope it would all blow over.

Someone eventually pointed out that I too had spent time with Keith. They asked me what I knew about it. I was terrified. If the hateful labels applied to him, then maybe they applied to me too. I denied everything. In an attempt to prove my innocence, I repeated the venomous rhetoric I had heard. I didn't know whom to trust, and I wasn't sure that I hadn't done something wrong. The older boy had made it stop, but I hadn't. Perhaps what had happened was my fault after all. I was drowning in feelings of guilt, hurt and confusion.

In the days that followed, I didn't know how to respond. I decided that the best defense was to try not to be noticed. Not to be good. Not to be a leader. Not to have potential. I just wanted to be invisible. I feared authority. I resisted leadership.

My weakened faith in leadership was further undermined by the anger and antagonism vented upon me by a succession of youth pastors at the church who had high expectations for me. I rebelled. One Sunday in youth group, I was goofing off by clapping off-beat to a worship song. Suddenly, I was interrupted by a blow to the head. The youth pastor had snuck up behind me and smacked me in the back of the head. I was shocked and angry.

This was not the last of the blows. A few years later, yet another youth pastor resigned in disgrace after being caught sexually abusing high school girls. Then, another youth leader sought me out sexually. This time I was older and wiser in the ways of the world. I resisted firmly, he gave up and nothing ever came of it. But I was confused. Was I doing something wrong? Was I sending some kind of signal that invited this victimization? I was afraid. My fear of discovery and mistrust of leadership slowly morphed into a caustic and abiding anger and a lifestyle of deception.

While still attending church with my family, I lived a completely different life at school and on the streets. I started taking drugs with my friends at the age of twelve. When I was fourteen, I began to drink as well. As my moral decline continued, I started stealing when the opportunity presented itself.

On top of all this, I tried to overcome my insecurities by proving that I was a red-blooded American man. I hid behind my mask of supposed manliness. I projected toughness, strength and power to hide my fears, my weaknesses and feelings of inadequacy. I did whatever I could to make myself attractive to the opposite sex. I wanted them to want to be with me. My desire was to be desired. I learned how to manipulate and seduce. At the same time, I was afraid of true intimacy. I wanted them to want me, but once I knew I had them I would run for the hills.

CHAPTER 2

PAIN UPON PAIN

While these inner struggles were picking up speed, I continued to be tapped for leadership. I was hiding the pain and the anger as best as I knew how. The summer of my fourteenth year, I was invited to attend a special leadership development camp. We went to Yosemite Valley and camped for a week. We studied the Bible and did various activities designed to encourage us and to train us to lead. Because it was a leadership camp, we were given a fair amount of freedom within the confines of the campground.

One afternoon four of us boys decided to search for caves to explore or rocks to climb. We left camp and followed some signs toward the base of a steep cliff called Royal Arches. As we approached the cliff, one of the boys decided to head back to camp for some reason. The three of us continued and started climbing over the loose stones and small boulders at the base of the cliff face. We were looking for caves, but couldn't find any. We started to climb up the face. Tom led the way, as he had done a little climbing before. He was also the tallest and could find the handholds more easily. Mark followed, and I brought up the rear.

It was late in the afternoon when we started climbing. With the sense of invincibility that only teenage boys have, we crammed our fingers into cracks, slid across narrow ledges and found chimneys to climb. We did all this without any equipment, training or supervision. Soon, we were a hundred feet or so off the ground. We realized we were high but thought that it wouldn't take us that long to climb the rest of the way up. After all, we had made it this far pretty quickly, or so we thought.

We continued to climb up and up. As the sun began to set and shadows started stretching across the valley, we realized we were in a tough spot. We knew that we either needed to get up or down the mountain quickly. Each passing minute left less of the mountain in the light and more covered by the rapidly encroaching shadows.

We decided to go up rather than down, thinking it would be safer. We thought we would be able to find an easy trail down the backside of the mountain. We were also much closer to the top than the bottom by this point. It wasn't long before we came to some tricky spots. Eventually, even we, the invincible ones, had to admit we could go no further up.

We paused for an impromptu conference on the side of the mountain and discussed the trouble we would be in for missing dinner and being late to the evening meeting. Having no way up, we decided we would have to climb back down. It was already dark, so there was no use in hurrying. We rested for a bit and then started down.

As we rested there on the face of the cliff, we heard people out in the valley singing and wondered if that was our group gathered around the fire. We heard people in the distance and the general hubbub of a campground. We knew we had better hurry down but were not sure of the best way to attempt it.

Our route up had been the result of haphazard guesswork. Retracing our steps was impossible. We were now going to have to find a safe way down in the absolute dark of a mountain night. During the last part of our upward climb, we had been going up a small stream running down a cleft in the rock we could get our hands in. After what had become hours of adventure, my fingers were numb from the cold and rubbed raw from the rock.

So, with our adrenaline flowing, we started down, picking our way along ledges and shimmying down cracks. We followed Tom as he felt around corners and swung out into the dark. Tom disappeared around a corner and called for Mark to follow him. Mark scooted out along a ledge that couldn't have been more than two inches wide. When he reached the corner, he slid his hand around and felt for something to grab.

There was nothing. Mark refused to go further. Tom reassured him that there was plenty of room on the ledge where he was now standing, but we couldn't see a thing. I volunteered to go around the corner next. Mark and I had to backtrack to where it was wide enough for us to change positions. We did this without any particular trouble.

As I made my way to the corner, Tom's disembodied voice called to me, offering reassurance. I stood with my back to the cliff and inched ever closer to the corner, the ledge narrowing as I went along. As I approached the corner, I felt around it and found nothing to hold on to. Tom told me that I was going to have to swing around the corner and that he would grab my hand and pull me to the ledge. He told me that he could see my hand but couldn't reach it until I swung around. It was just too far. There was no way back. So, I turned my right foot and dug my toe into what remained of the ledge where I stood. I gripped the corner with my right hand and swung my left foot and arm out into the darkness, hoping there was a ledge for me at the end of their arc.

Sure enough, the ledge was there, as was Tom. He and I agreed that it would be best for us to change places and for him to guide Mark around the corner. We had to climb down quite a distance before we found a place wide enough to switch. Tom went back up, while I waited on a ledge just wide enough for my feet turned parallel to the cliff face. It was three or four inches wide. Tom patiently coaxed Mark toward the corner. I called out that I had made it and I was sure that he would as well.

"Nothing to worry about! It's not as hard as it sounds! You can do it!" I called.

Mark was scared; you could hear it in his voice. Tom kept assuring him it would be fine. I still remember the panic in Mark's voice as he said, "Tom, I'm slipping!" I heard a slip, a bump, and felt a whoosh as something went by me. Just to my left, I heard a grunt. It was like the sound when the wind is knocked out of you.

I remember Tom calling out for Mark and then yelling that Mark had fallen. I remember Tom, in a near hysterical panic, scurrying down the mountain and suddenly appearing where I stood. We stood on that tiny ledge calling for Mark, yelling for Mark. When no answer came back, we started screaming for help. Tom was in a frenzy to find Mark and help him. I remember trying to pin him to the mountain and telling him to calm down because we couldn't help Mark if we fell too. We needed to calm down.

We spent the next while shouting for help. I don't know how long we screamed. We hoped our voices would carry at least as well as the sound of the campfire singing we had heard earlier. After a while, Tom decided no one was coming and that he would have to try to make it down. We didn't know where Mark was or what his condition was. I told him I didn't think I could make it down. I wasn't sure he should try either. He said that he wouldn't do anything foolish and that it didn't hurt to try. He would come back if he couldn't find his way down.

We decided that I would keep calling for help while Tom would try to make it to the bottom. Tom climbed across me and started down to my left. I edged along the ledge with him for a bit, and then we kept in contact as he made his way down. Just as he made it to the bottom, a light emerged at the edge of the forest near the base of the cliff. I called out to Tom to alert him that help had arrived.

Together, we told the ranger what had happened. He had a radio and called for help. He approached the foot of the cliff about 75 feet below me. For a brief moment, his flashlight lingered upon the bloodied body of my friend, Mark. The ranger was back on the radio then, more frantically and with renewed urgency. I couldn't make out anything he was saying.

Tom had planned to guide me down. He assured the ranger that it was easy compared to other things we had done that afternoon. The ranger wouldn't have it. He told me to stay put. I didn't need much convincing. I was cold and very tired. Soon more lights arrived, and a canopy was set up over Mark. I continually called down to find out how he was doing. Always the same response: "As well as can be expected." Someone was constantly talking to me and reassuring me for the next several hours.

Finally, around four in the morning, I heard someone coming down the mountain above me. It turned out that it was easier for the rangers to hike up the backside of the mountain and rappel down to where I was than to attempt any other kind of rescue. When the ranger got to me, my hands wouldn't release from the rock. I couldn't let go. They had to pry my fingers loose.

When I got down, medics examined me and found blood on my hands. I thought I must have cut my hands on the rocks in the dark, but as they washed my hands, they found blood and hair, but no cuts, just scratches. It wasn't my blood. I kept asking to see Mark, but they said they had to move him and that they needed to get me back to camp. A few minutes later, in the back of a ranger's car, I learned that he was dead. Apparently, he was dead before he even reached the bottom. He had hit his head on the outcrop that had become my handhold and never regained consciousness. I had spent the last several hours clinging to the rock that had been the death of him. It had been his blood on my hands.

I struggled with guilt. I was wracked with it. *Why had Mark died? Why not me? Tom was taller. Mark was stronger. Why had I survived?* "What if" questions haunted me. *What if we hadn't made the climb? What if we had stopped and waited? What if?* There were questions upon questions.

Over the next few weeks, the whole world seemed to want to hear the story. I felt sick inside. One Sunday after church, Mark's parents told me that God had a purpose for my life and that they were glad I had not died. I broke down sobbing in their arms, repeatedly saying how sorry I was. Only now, years later, with children of my own, do I begin to understand how difficult that moment must have been for them.

I remember the funeral. I remember trying to figure out what people wanted from me. I remember being told that it all happened for a purpose. I remember trying to play the part of the faith-filled young man, all the while feeling empty, sad and angry. I remember the platitudes that always seemed to leave me with more questions, not fewer, feeling worse, not better. I remember being told that God is working out His good purposes and that I should trust Him and never question His wisdom, His plan. I think I tried to stop the questions, or at least to avoid them. I had new hurts, pain on top of pain. I didn't know which way to turn.

All the while, I went to church at least twice a week. At first, I kept up the façade. I pretended to believe. Then it dawned on me that perhaps everyone else was just pretending as well. Perhaps no one really believed. Maybe it was all a sham. After all, God didn't protect me from abuse. People who professed to believe in God were the abusers. God, Christians and Christianity became the target for my scorn and bitterness. I watched as church leaders fell. My convictions grew stronger. *These Christians are all talk, I thought. They are all a bunch of hypocrites! Where are the ones with true faith?!*

By the time we were in high school, my friends and I would sneak out of church to go drinking. We openly mocked the more righteous in the youth group and, much to my disgrace, took great relish in corrupting others. As I look back, I recognize myself in Paul's words to the Romans: "Although they know God's righteous decree that those who do such things deserve death, they not only continue to do these very things but also approve of those who practice them." I was an antagonist of the truth and an active recruiter to drunkenness, drugs and debauchery.

I continued on this way, dabbling with different drugs and girls for years. I didn't know it at the time, but I was running from the pain and shame. All the while, the very things I was doing to try to escape were heaping more guilt and shame on me. I knew I didn't really care about the girls I used. I knew the drugs and alcohol were dangerous and wrong. I used words and anger to control people and situations. I developed a filthy mouth and cursed so much that I hardly knew when I was doing it. Lies came out of my mouth more quickly and easily than the truth. My speech was toxic, steeped with sarcasm and malicious mocking.

One of the interesting things about this season was that, in the midst of these years of depravity, I felt conviction. Even at the time, I marvelled at my companions in crime. They could do all the same things I did, but apparently never struggle with guilt. I always woke up the next morning feeling terrible. I questioned my friends, probing to see how they felt about our actions. The next day as they retold the stories with relish, I would cringe inside at the things I did, the things I said. I felt bad. I knew it was wrong and that there was more to life than this, but I couldn't find it, or I couldn't face it.

My only explanation for my inability to freely enjoy my debauchery is that the Spirit was alive and active in my soul. He wouldn't let me get away. As I look back, I see the way the Holy Spirit was wooing me and working in and around me. Even as I ran from Him, He saved me. He prevented my death more times than I can clearly recall. He was calling to me through the haze of pain and escapism. He was pursuing me. The hound of heaven was on my trail. I fled him.

He wanted to deal with the pain in my heart—pain that had become a sort of boil in my soul, too sore to touch. I know now that lancing an infected wound is a step toward healing. At that time, I was too scared to let anyone get close to me. Like a wounded animal backed into a corner, I lashed out at anyone foolish enough to get close to me. But God is just that kind of wonderful fool. Jesus steps toward the blows and took my lashes. He is big enough to handle my ranting. If only I had understood then. At the time, I could not imagine healing. I refused to admit that anything was wrong. I was in denial.

The central question for me at the time became one of control. *Who is in control? Who has the power?* I was afraid of someone else being in control. I was determined not to be taken in again, or to let another person have power over me. I didn't want to be fooled again. So, I chose rebellion and rejected submission in any form. I didn't trust. I couldn't trust—not myself or anyone else. I was determined not to be hurt again, but I was my own worst enemy.

I was sure the world was full of predators and prey. I wasn't going to be the prey again. I tricked, used and victimized others, but this too was useless and brought no relief. I was full of false bravado, but inside I was a scared little boy who just wanted to be OK. I just couldn't find the way to OK. I wanted to be loved, but this desire had become so twisted, so sexual.

Starting with the pornographic images of my childhood, my mind had been warped to think of intimacy primarily in sexual terms. Sex was the great secret, the driving factor. This was constantly reaffirmed everywhere around me. In my world, love was lust. Intimacy was sex. If someone desired me, wanted me, I was OK.

A picture of a woman offering herself to the camera became a cheap and addictive substitute for real intimacy. I could imagine myself the object of her feigned desire. I felt OK because I could "have her." I was swimming in a heady mix of flesh and fantasy that was only limited by my ability to find fresh meat to feed the beast. The simulated intimacy belied the real intimacy of soul I was searching for. I wanted to be desired, known and loved completely.

The great irony of all this is that someone *does* know us completely and offers Himself to us freely. He shares the secret places of His heart with us. He delights in us. He declares Himself our Lover. He rejoices over us and composes love songs to us. He loves us in beauty and poetry as well as with a fierce and active love that is more than just words or images. He demonstrated His love for us in the most concrete terms. When we were still rejecting Him, He laid down His very life for us, not just figuratively but literally. He ransomed us back. He paid the debt. Of course, I didn't understand any of this then. I was running.

I was trying to distance myself from the pain, and this meant I had to get away from myself. I was trying to hide from myself and from God. All through this period, I was still attending church. My parents required me to go to church until I turned eighteen. Every Sunday, whether I liked it or not, I was in church. More often than I would like to admit, they dragged me out of bed with a hangover and trundled me off to church. While I certainly didn't appreciate this at the time, at least I was consistently being exposed to the Scriptures. On some level, I think I knew I was looking for something, but I was sure that it wasn't to be found among the hypocrites and abusers, among the Christians. I continued my search, looking for new experiences, new drugs, new ideas and more forbidden fruit to taste. The last drug I took was LSD.

I took this drug several times over a couple of months when I was eighteen. While I was on it the first time, I was sure I had figured out life and the meaning of the universe. I thought I had seen beyond the surface of things and figured out that everything was part of a unified mystery. I was sure all the philosophers, prophets, mystics and religious teachers were saying the same thing.

The fact that this "revelation" came to me in a drug-induced state didn't bother me in the least. I shared this experience with my friend Robert. We spent the next couple of months reading and dropping acid to further develop our insight into the religion behind all religions. We read philosophy and searched the sacred texts of the major religions, seeking to reconcile them with one another.

Our project was coming along nicely until one day Robert tried to bring Jesus into the mix. I was sitting in the dining room at my house talking to Robert on the telephone. We were waxing eloquent about Prince Siddhartha, Marx and Muhammad. Robert said that they were all pointing to the same ideas but were expressing them in words that would make sense to the people within their particular time and culture. I agreed.

"They never claimed to be God," Robert said. "They just claimed to know the way to God, or enlightenment, or whatever you want to call it."

I agreed.

"After all," Robert continued, "even Jesus didn't claim to be God!"

Oops.

This is where the Sunday school lessons started coming back to me. This is where my father's encouragement to be intellectually honest and a critical thinker forced me into a corner. I couldn't let Robert's comment pass. I stopped him.

"Actually, I think He did."

He was surprised to hear that Jesus had made such a claim and questioned me about it. I set down the phone and quickly searched my bedroom for my neglected but not forgotten Bible. I returned to the living room and explained to Robert what Jesus claimed about Himself. I flipped through the Gospels, reading relevant sections over the phone—the sections in which Jesus said that He was the only way to God, and that He and the Father are one.

Robert tried to explain away the sayings as misunderstanding or later corruptions of the text. I knew too much to let him get away with that. We had to be honest in our pursuit of truth or we were no better than the other shysters and religious hypocrites. Robert was noticeably disappointed that Jesus, and therefore Christianity, didn't seem to fit with our theory. I was disquieted as well. I could make sense of and therefore dismiss all the others, but not Jesus.

As it turned out, my mother had overheard my conversation with Robert from the next room. She made no attempt to hide her surprise at what had just transpired. When I hung up, she asked me if I realized that I had been "witnessing" to him. I was mortified and embarrassed. I made a sarcastic remark about how I didn't even believe it myself and was only answering his questions. That shut down the conversation quickly but didn't stop me from wondering about Jesus. *Could it be true? Could it be that Jesus truly is who He claimed to be?*

CHAPTER 3

STIRRINGS

Not long after that conversation with Robert, I had another eventful conversation. My brother and I were smoking pot together, and I made an off-handed remark that sent him into near hysterical laughter. (I find it odd, and more than a little ironic, that the Lord used even my drug-laced conversations and drug-induced experiences to bring me to Himself. He was there with me though I knew it not.) The thing I said that drove my brother into fits of laughter was that I wasn't a "drug user." I was just "experimenting with drugs."

My brother found that absolutely hilarious because I had been "experimenting with drugs" for roughly six years at that time. He pointed out, in rather ruthless logic, that you don't "experiment with drugs" for six years. Experimenting meant trying something once or twice, but after all this time, I couldn't use that phrase any more. I was a drug user.

That was a shock to my self-image! I liked the neon-lighted MTV picture of experimentation better than the harsh journalistic glare of the documentary on drug use. It all sounded so cool to be experimenting with drugs, but the "drug user" label conjured up a very different picture. Drug users were addicts. Drug users were out of control. Drug users were losers. I didn't like that picture.

I much preferred the idea that I was just a young person doing what a "normal" young person does: experimenting with sex, drugs and rock 'n' roll. That one conversation jolted me out of my denial and forced me to face the unpleasant realities of what I had become. I realized that several of my friends were in jail, rehab or the cemetery. I realized that I was actually a drug user and that the road I was on was leading me to a bad place.

So, I stopped.

One day, I decided I didn't want to do it anymore, and I simply stopped. I don't know how I did it. I know it doesn't work this way for everyone, but I just stopped. I soon found that hanging out with my partying friends wasn't any fun if I wasn't drunk, stoned or at least mildly inebriated. I didn't enjoy being with them, and although I never said anything, I believe they felt judged by my not joining in. Substance abuse is not a spectator sport.

They actively recruited me to re-engage in the partying life and were offended, and sometimes abusive, when I wouldn't. We had all helped each other off the wagon many times before. This time was different for me. This wasn't just a "morning after" pledge to never drink again after a night of vomiting. Something was stirring in me, and I was put off by what once enthralled me.

The pleasures of the path I had chosen helped to numb the pain in my heart for several years. However, the methods I used to find escape from dealing with my own heart were no longer effective. I now understand that my loving Father God was drawing me to Himself. He was allowing me to see the ugliness of the lovers I was entwined with. He was offering me something better. The growing discontent in my own heart was actually a gift from God to spur me on again to pursue Him. The search wasn't futile; I had just been looking in all the wrong places.

Without partying to keep me busy, I had lots of time to think. I started to feel the pain, to feel the emptiness inside. Now that I was no longer attempting to numb the ache with drugs or alcohol, the pain was worse. I continued the search for truth that Robert and I had begun, this time on my own. I kept reading. I no longer spent much time with my drug friends and had no friend besides them. As those friendships started to wither, I grew lonely.

My parents noticed I was no longer going out with my friends. I don't know if they had known about the drug use, or that I had stopped using. I suspect they noticed differences in me. They started asking me why I didn't go out with my friends any more. I think they may have worried about this new, dark loneliness as much as they had about the bad company I had been hanging out with before.

I went to work and to class at the college but spent the rest of my time largely alone. In my relative solitude, I read and pondered. I kept wondering about the big questions: *Why am I here? What does any of this mean?* I investigated existentialism and communism. I toyed with Buddhism and New Age philosophy. I was willing to consider just about any religion or philosophy of life other than Christianity.

I knew Christianity was a sham. I knew they were all liars and hypocrites, abusers and criminals—or at the very least, narrow-minded, ignorant, kindhearted fools. I was no longer attending church at this point since my parents no longer required it after I turned eighteen. I fancied myself emancipated but was more burdened and confused than ever.

I don't recall exactly how it happened, but one day I picked up my Bible and started reading it. I vaguely remember thinking that I had investigated everything else, and that I had to at least investigate Christianity to be intellectually honest in my rejection of it. Little did I know that the hound of heaven was closing in.

Soon after that, I got a call from one of the pastors at my parents' church. He invited me to go to the mountains for the weekend with the youth. After learning that the retreat would cost several hundred dollars, I declined the invitation. I also told him, in no uncertain terms, that I wasn't interested in God, church or hanging out with Christians. He was casual in his response, but did mention that he would be willing to pay my way if I changed my mind.

As the weekend approached, I found myself feeling bored and lonely. I decided to take advantage of the pastor's offer. A free trip to the mountains sounded better than sitting home alone. I told him I would go, but that I wouldn't sit through any preaching or meetings. He agreed to my conditions. On the day of the retreat, I showed up at the church looking every inch the sullen malcontent that I was.

Throughout the weekend, I kept my earphones on as much as possible, trying to avoid talking with people. Each day after breakfast, I would disappear. I spent the days on long hikes in the mountains with just my Walkman and my Bible. There, looking out over the valley, I read the biblical accounts of the life of Jesus while listening to Bob Marley and Jimi Hendrix. I only rejoined the group when I made it to meals or returned to the cabin at night. I can only imagine what the others thought about my antisocial behavior that weekend. I'm sure it didn't look good.

Nevertheless, it was on that weekend, in the midst of my outwardly rebellious behavior, that I finally inwardly surrendered to God. I was sitting high on a mountain overlooking the valley below. I read the Gospel of John and sat there with tears streaming down my face. I struggled—truly wrestled—with the truth. Jesus was the crux of the issue. If He really lived and really died, if He really was who He said He was, that would settle the issue. I knew I needed help. I knew I needed a Savior, but I was afraid to trust, to be taken in only to be wounded again.

I didn't want to believe. I didn't want to admit I had been wrong for so many years. I didn't want to humble myself, to give up control. I especially didn't want to become a Christian. I hated Christians. But there, on that mountain, I told Jesus that I believed. I told Him that I was tired of fighting Him and that I would follow Him the rest of my days. I surrendered.

I recognized that the longings of my soul, my thirst, would never be quenched apart from the true and living God. I saw that the restlessness in my soul could only be stilled by the presence of God. I didn't have these words for it at the time, but I was finally responding to the gentle but persistent knocking on the door of my heart. Jesus had been waiting at the door, and I finally invited Him in.

There was no thunder. No lightning. There was no immediate or recognizable change in behavior. I returned to the cabin and told no one what had happened. The next day we went down the mountain, and still I told no one. It was another couple of weeks before I mustered the courage to tell my parents what had happened. They were nonchalant about it. That was the perfect response.

They loved me and gave me space to explore my burgeoning belief. I was embarrassed by my faith and not at all sure I wanted to embrace Christianity, even though I had embraced Christ. I believed in Jesus and wanted to know Him, but I wasn't at all sure about His people.

I was frustrated by the superior responses of others as the news of my conversion began to get out. I was humiliated as they pointed out that they had been right all along and I had been wrong. I was angry when they told me they had prayed for me to see the light. Their superior smiles and self-satisfied stares were almost too much! Still, I couldn't go back. Jesus was God. It was undeniable truth. It was the only right way of understanding life, the universe and everything. Where could I go? What could I do?

I was caught by the truth. I couldn't deny I had been wrong. I couldn't deny that He was actually God. If God was now my Father then these patronizing and unintentionally antagonizing Christians were now my brothers and sisters. I couldn't love Him and hate them at the same time. That was probably the hardest part for me about coming to faith. I was ready to humble myself before God, but humbling myself before people was much more difficult!

One of the rich blessings I received at this time came through two of the pastors at the church. Not long after I told my parents, I told the pastor who had paid for my trip to the mountains. He smiled and asked me to join him and a young pastor in meeting together once a week. We talked about life, read the Scriptures and prayed together. These men welcoming me into their friendship was what eased me back into church.

They were on my side, and that helped me a lot. They let me honestly wrestle with questions and weren't quick to offer easy advice and oversimplified wisdom. They helped me search the Scriptures and encouraged me to search for God at my own pace. These men honestly lived out their relationship with God before me and invited me to do the same. This was an invaluable gift to me as a young believer.

I was experiencing the joy of real fellowship with the people of God. Growing up in the church left me with only a vague sense of what fellowship was, and most of that was associated with coffee and doughnuts or potluck dinners. With these two men I began to experience real community, real connection.

Within just a few months, these pastors asked me to join them in working with young people at the church. So, less than six months after giving my life to Christ, at the age of nineteen, I got involved in ministry. It started with going to mid-week youth meetings, the same kind of meetings I had tried so hard to avoid just a few years earlier. Then, I started meeting each week with a couple of junior high school students on my own. I felt as if I was just a few steps ahead of these boys. I was amazed they would want to meet with me. Soon, I was teaching at the mid-week meetings and learning to play guitar so I could help lead the singing.

My involvement in ministry so quickly after surrendering to Jesus accelerated my growth in some areas. As I was teaching, I was also learning. I found that teaching forced me to learn. I found that leading others forced me to keep moving forward in my relationship with Him. I was constantly in over my head, and this propelled me into dependence on God.

My rapid ascent into leadership forced me to grow spiritually, but it played upon a hidden weakness as well. Teaching and leading opened up new paths to affirmation and respect. I was developing a new addiction. I began to drink in the respect of those around me. I found that people responded to my teaching and leadership. This met a deep need in my soul. I craved respect and tried to fill this void by excelling in ministry.

My addiction to affirmation was more acceptable and therefore more insidious than drugs and alcohol. I could quench my soul thirst with the applause of people. No one goes to rehab because of the praise of men. I could get my fix in public. No one dies from approval. But this addiction was just as dangerous for my soul.

I had spent many years developing habits of thought and wearing ruts into the pathways of my mind. I was used to looking for love in all the wrong places. As I was developing my new addiction to praise, I was continuing in my addiction to lust and pornography. Unlike my addiction to drugs, I had no sudden breakthrough in this area. In fact, perhaps the only thing that kept this addiction from going further was my fear of discovery. I told myself the same lies each time: *No one needs to know. No one will ever know. Just this one last time.*

I was living a double life. I still wanted to be desired. I was still searching for intimacy. I was becoming one of the hypocrites I had hated. It didn't help that when I shared my struggles with other young men in our church, I was largely met with a chorus of "me too." I found that nearly every man I met struggled with the same thing, or rather failed at the same thing.

There is a world of difference between struggling against temptation and giving in to sin. It wasn't that we were wrestling with our inner demons and winning, but rather that we were dancing with them and bemoaning our fate. Rather than helping one another out of the mess, we were validating the mess for each other. None of us knew a way out.

I had a new foundation, in Christ, but there was much demolition yet to be done on the structure of my life. My basic orientation had changed, but I was still wounded. I didn't know which way to turn.

CHAPTER 4

I STILL HAVEN'T FOUND WHAT I'M LOOKING FOR

I felt a bit like a dog that finally catches a car he's been chasing and then doesn't know what to do with it. I had resisted Christ for so long! Despite my best efforts, I had been dragged kicking and screaming into the Kingdom of God. I had new life in Christ but I didn't know how to overcome the problems around me or, more importantly, within me. When you have already found "the answer," how can you continue to ask questions? When the deepest needs of your soul have been met in Christ, how can you still have a longing in your soul?

As time went on, I was increasingly confused about what was supposed to happen next. As I got to know Jesus through the Word, through prayer, through worship, through service and through life, I started to change. It was a good change. I was becoming a different version of myself, a better version. I was experiencing more lightness, freedom and joy than I had imagined possible. I smiled more, joked more, felt more confidence and liberty than I had ever known; but beneath the surface, there was still an ache—a pain that lurked within.

As I vented my frustration and voiced my questions to a few friends, they seemed to be caught off guard.

"Just believe," they would tell me. "Jesus is the way the truth and the life."

"I believe that," I told them. "But there is still the problem with the porn! What am I supposed to do with that? Believe harder? Have more faith? I would get more faith if I knew where to buy it! How do you believe more, harder or stronger?"

I found myself crying out like the man with the sick child in Mark 9:24: "I do believe; help me overcome my unbelief!"

I wondered if the Christian life was easier for other people. I thought maybe I was one of the few who persistently struggled with sin. It seemed I was surrounded by shiny happy people. I wondered if I was the only damaged one. *Am I the only one whom the answer leaves with more questions? Maybe I am just more damaged than my friends and peers.* I just couldn't make it work for me. The more I got to know Christ, the more I felt that there must be more available. I had found Him, but still hadn't found what I was looking for.

Then, I remembered my friends were struggling too. They were just as messed up as I was. In quiet moments, they would share their questions and struggles with me. But they knew better than to raise them publicly. They had learned the rules of the game. They had learned how to play church better than I had. I'm still not very good at it.

The church in which I was raised spent a lot of time encouraging evangelism and inviting people to come to Jesus, to repent and be baptized. We talked about the good news, and we bemoaned the fate of those who rejected God. We were concerned for the lost, and we wanted people to get saved.

"Whatever your question," we were assured, "Jesus is the answer."

It's not that this is entirely wrong. I know these pithy sayings express some aspect of the truth. But my experience tells me that, even after knowing Jesus, many equations remain unsolved.

The basic orientation of the church was toward truth and the belief that if you know the truth, then the truth will set you free. But I knew I wasn't free. I knew that many others weren't free either. I studied the Scriptures and even taught others. I was learning, but I longed for something beyond knowledge, something more like experience, something more like freedom. I searched for true guidance but got clichéd advice instead.

Once, while talking with a man I respected, I told him I was longing for more.

"There is no more," he replied. "You just believe in Jesus and do the right thing."

I was so discouraged. The problem is that I tried to do the right thing. Try as I might, I couldn't consistently choose the right thing. I was told to read the Bible more. I was told to pray more. I was told to memorize Scripture. I was told that service and pouring yourself into ministry was the answer. I tried these solutions and, to be honest, they did help in some ways. I got to know the Bible, and more importantly, I got to know Jesus better. But at the end of the day, I felt horrible as my secret sins continued, and guilt piled on with no solution in sight.

Half-truths are more dangerous than bald-faced lies. I know these people meant well. I am sure they were giving me the best advice they knew, but they only knew half the story themselves. It is true that once you have been adopted into the family of God, you don't have to be adopted again. You have, at your point of conversion, as much of Jesus as you are ever going to get. But it is also true that there is more to be learned, more to be healed, more growth to be experienced.

I was being sold a vision of life with Christ that required me to hang on tight and "white-knuckle it" until heaven. I wanted more. I wanted the eternal kind of life here on earth. I was pretty sure Jesus had promised that, but I was nowhere near experiencing it. I don't think many people I knew were either. I was still searching, but they had given up hope. Many of them claimed a level of satisfaction and joy that wasn't evident in their lives.

They were in denial, claiming that every day with Jesus was sweeter than the day before, while gritting their teeth and facing their trials and temptations alone. Others readily admitted their problems, but they seemed to wear their sins and failures as a badge of authenticity. They offered no solutions either. So, with no other options in sight, I just ploughed on, trying harder.

I didn't know it, but I was steadily moving down the path to pharisaical pride and legalism. I was caught in a trap. The more Scripture I memorized and the more times I taught, the more confident I became that I needed to convince others. I guess I thought that if I could convince others, I would be well on my way to being convinced myself.

As I continued college, I got more and more involved in ministry as well as my studies. Having been raised in a family in which argumentation was an art form, I found I excelled at apologetics, the art of intellectually defending Christianity. I loved a good argument and was ready to research. I devoured books and looked for opportunities to present what I was learning. I loved to debate, to engage in the struggle for truth. My success in these arenas brought me accolades and met my need to be respected but did nothing to help me find the peace and freedom that were eluding me.

During this time, I was going to school, volunteering at church and working in a warehouse. I was living with my parents, and our relationship was better than ever. My job gave me plenty of opportunities to compare what I was learning at church with the real world. The men and women I worked with weren't particularly better or worse than anyone else. They were a good cross section of society. I got along well with everyone and looked for opportunities to demonstrate the love of Jesus in word and deed.

I found I could develop real, honest relationships with these people as easily as I could at church—perhaps more easily. I believe God used me to show His love to some of them. There was the drug-addicted hippie who invited me to come to dinner to talk about Jesus with his wife and kids. There was the transgender friend who encouraged me to start a church. She said she would go to it if I did. I invited her to come with me to the church I was attending, but she declined. I didn't understand why. (In hindsight, I suspect she had a more realistic understanding than I did of how she would be received in a church setting.)

One evening, I arrived home from work to a dark and quiet house. I was somewhat surprised when no one was home, as our house was generally a hive of activity. Before I could get my key in the front door, I was approached by one of the neighbors. He said he'd seen me drive up and had been waiting for me to get home. He told me my family was at the hospital.

My father had suffered a seizure. An ambulance had taken him to the emergency room. My neighbor wasn't very clear on the details but was very kind in his concern. I must have been visibly shaken as he offered to drive me to the hospital. I took him up on his offer and peppered him with questions on the way, questions for which he had no answers.

When we arrived at the hospital, I hurried inside to find my mother and sister with several good friends of the family. The crisis wasn't even hours old, but the Body of Christ had already started caring for its wounded members. We waited for what seemed an eternity until the doctors called us. They wanted the family to come in, and so we all went back.

The doctor was confused by the number of people, and my mother assured him that these members of the church were our family. The doctor then put a couple of X-rays up on a light box and showed us images of a golf ball-sized tumor in my father's head and a fist-sized tumor in his chest. He explained that my father probably had about three weeks to live. My mother asked him a few questions, and we all stood there for a moment.

The doctor began to look perplexed and asked us if we understood what he was telling us. I assured him that we did and repeated back to him all the things we had heard him say. This left him looking even more confused. Why were we were taking this devastating news so calmly? My mother explained to him that we knew Christ. While we were troubled, we were also filled with peace because we knew that God had the whole situation under control. I still remember him shaking his head in disbelief as he walked away.

I truly believe we were experiencing supernatural grace and peace from God. We weren't pretending to be peaceful. We actually *were* peaceful. I can't explain it other than that. God gave us peace when we needed it. The pain would come later.

I called my brother from a pay phone in the lobby. He was living in another state at the time. I told him about the situation and encouraged him to come home as quickly as possible. He was back 36 hours later, having driven straight through with a friend. With the family gathered, we faced the challenge of cancer. As it turns out, the emergency room doctor was wrong in the prognosis, if not in the diagnosis.

The cancer was advanced but potentially operable, not inoperable as he had thought. A few days later, after eight hours of surgery, the surgeon said my father had a chance of survival if they also pursued aggressive chemotherapy and radiation treatments. My father responded well to the treatments. Within a few months, he was well enough to consider returning to work.

We all tried to fill in the gaps and help. We were all tired and experiencing a lot of stress. Tempers occasionally flared. We loved each other and made it through the best we could. When my dad started working again, I pursued transferring to a university to finish my studies. Just before I was to leave to continue my education hundreds of miles away, the cancer came back. My father started to deteriorate again. This time there was no operation, no treatment options. The cancer was back with a vengeance, and there was only one possible ending.

I assumed this meant I'd need to hold off on going away to university, but my father disagreed. The discussion went back and forth. He insisted that the best way for me to love him and support him was to continue with my life and studies. He said he didn't want me to put my life on hold for "some macabre death watch." He said it would give him joy to know I was moving forward with my life. I didn't want to go. I felt they needed me, that he needed me. He assured me they had all the help they needed. I couldn't argue with that as I had seen the Body rally around us, and so my father's argument prevailed.

I don't know if I have ever seen a more beautiful expression of the Body of Christ than what I witnessed during those years of my father's illness. The people of our church gathered around our family and supported us in so many ways, practical and tangible, as well as emotional and spiritual. People whom I had judged, feared—and at times even hated— loved and served us.

They demonstrated the love of Christ to us in incredible ways. I don't know how many meals they brought to us. I don't know how many rides to the doctor, shoulders to cry on or small acts of kindness we received: The family of painters who painted our house when we needed it. The men coming in the evenings straight from work just to sit with my father. These few episodes don't begin to convey the amazing love with which the people of the church enveloped our family.

All this love was like a salve to my soul. These were messed up and broken people, but they were the people of God. With all their prejudices and fears, all their foibles and flaws, they were His hands and feet. How could I continue to hold them at arm's length when they loved us so well? How could I explain their love? I had seen their failures. I heard the stories and knew all about church politics. As a leader in the church, my father had engaged in some intense arguments with a few of them. But here they were with a casserole in hand and a kind word for my mother.

Of course, they offered many of the same gut-wrenching platitudes, the same advice to "just trust God." But somehow, there was less sting in words like these when they were accompanied by such empathy expressed in tandem with obvious love and concern. They weren't perfect, but they were my family. They were there to care for my father while I was away at university.

CHAPTER 5

FALLING FORWARD

It was a confusing time for me as I felt pulled in a number of conflicting directions. I was growing in my relationship with God and was experiencing more peace and happiness than I had ever known, but I continued to struggle with purity. I also continued to find my identity in the respect of others. I still harbored some anger toward church and was skeptical of leaders, even as I saw the love of Christ expressed clearly through some of the Christians around us. As my father's life was moving inexorably towards the end, I was studying at one of the best universities in the country and launching out into a life of my own.

There is something of the ridiculous in my attendance at the University of California, Berkeley. I didn't really want to go there at all. I had applied to two universities, Berkeley and one not as highly regarded, but much closer to home. When my dad got sick again, I had decided I would go to the closer one. I was frustrated and confused when I was rejected. This was even more surprising because I had been enrolled in a program at the local community college that guaranteed acceptance and a seamless transfer to that particular university. I was angry, but I felt a little better when I discovered I had been accepted at Berkeley. This came as a bit of a shock to all of us. So, with no other option available to me, I made plans to attend a university I had never dreamed I would get into.

In hindsight, I recognize that this was a pivotal point in my journey. If I'd had the option, I would not have chosen this path. I am so glad that my loving Father, who knows the end from the beginning, didn't give me a choice. So many things in my journey flow from my attendance at Berkeley. God intervened again to direct me on the path that would lead me to Him. I didn't see any of this at the time, but even then, I recognized it was nearly miraculous that I would end up at a university of that stature.

Berkeley generally takes in only the finest of students with outstanding grades and extracurricular accomplishments. I had not been a very dedicated student in high school. My grades were not great by any stretch, and my extracurricular activities were not the sort one would put on paper when applying to colleges.

My parents always believed that I was capable of much more than I produced. There were many lectures at home about my lack of drive. Always the monster of potential lurked in the background. A saving grace was that I generally did very well on standardized tests. My parents had watched me decline from a motivated and successful child, to a sullen and withdrawn teenager doing just enough to get by.

Based on my test scores, I was singled out for enrollment in a special college preparatory high school program. Even there, I didn't live up to expectations. I managed to cheat or cajole my way through my classes. I generally did the bare minimum to squeeze by. I had no plans to attend university after high school. I had no plans of any kind. These were the hazy years of drugs and partying. I was more interested in virtually any form of escape than I was in studying. Many of my friends, who were more interested in education than partying, if only marginally so, made plans to attend excellent universities around the country.

I spent most of the summer after graduating from high school partying with my friends. Then, one by one, they started to head off to universities around the country. One morning, my mother knocked on my bedroom door and we had another conversation about my potential and my future. She had heard from a friend that classes were starting at our local community college that very morning. She encouraged me to see if I could still enroll. I had nothing better to do that day, so I drove over to the campus. I was none too motivated but somehow I found myself standing in front of the administration building at the college.

I don't know exactly how it all happened, but by the end of the week, I was enrolled in an honors program and had a full schedule of classes. I even received a small scholarship to cover the already low tuition and my books. I was out of excuses. So began my pursuit of a higher education—hardly an enthusiastic beginning.

It was in that first semester that my spiritual thirst surfaced and my search for truth began. That was when I was spending time with Robert, writing our own religion. I quit using drugs toward the end of that semester. The trip to the mountains and my embrace of Christ came a few months after that.

A year and a half after starting classes at the community college, I had enough units to transfer to a four-year university. I wanted to major in history, and I suddenly found myself attending the highest rated history department in the country, at Berkeley. I had only chosen history as a major because it came easily to me. Again, I had chosen the path of least resistance.

I still look back in amazement at how I stumbled from one ill-considered choice to another, and how God worked it all out for my good. Sometimes, I feel like I've been sleepwalking through my life, falling forward. The Father has been so patient to walk alongside me and to guide me into the path that is best for me, despite myself. I only vaguely saw His hand in it at the time.

It was a heady time as I moved away to Berkeley. I rented an apartment just off campus and started a new life. I had a few friends at the university, but they were all from my old life. I had maintained contact with them and had even visited a few times for parties before I had embraced Christ. It was strange to realize that I had driven hundreds of miles to attend drug and alcohol-fueled parties at this place. Now that I was actually going to live here, I was embarking on a very new chapter of life

When my friends heard I had been accepted at the university, they prepared a warm welcome; however, I had changed since I last saw them. The person they knew was no more, or at least was in the process of transformation. It was a new man, a different one, who arrived and moved in up the street. This caused some real confusion as I resisted their invitations to get drunk or stoned.

In the meantime, I was looking for some Christians to spend time with. I had experienced the benefits of growing in community, but I didn't know a single Christian on campus. My first attempt was a bit of a disaster. I unwittingly started attending a "Christian" Bible study that turned out to be a cult. I knew enough to recognize that something was wrong, but it was a few weeks before the whole picture came into focus. It wasn't too difficult to extricate myself, as they were happy to shun me. They cut off all contact I had with anyone in the group, lest I cause one of them to "fall away." After that unpleasant experience, I wasn't too keen to join another group.

Eventually, I came across a Christian student fellowship that had chapters around the world. I had heard of it before and felt safe enough to try it out. I soon found myself on the inside and was invited into leadership. Most of the students, and even many of the staff, had come to faith in the last few years. Very few of them had come from the kind of church or family background I had. My grasp of biblical data propelled my rise to leadership.

The group had a strong emphasis on evangelism and discipleship and a very clear, if somewhat rigid, program to promote it. We were strongly encouraged to share our faith using particular methods and tools. We were expected to progress through a series of studies that, when completed, would yield certain results in our lives: a strong foundation and a true disciple. I was progressing quickly through the program and was feeling pretty self-satisfied. I was puffed up with my knowledge and performance.

During this time, I was introduced to a friend of a friend. Jason was a first year student and I was a couple of years ahead of him. He was new in town and needed a friend. When I discovered he wasn't a Christian, I was eager to befriend him and evangelize him.

I was sure he needed Christ. I was also sure that I was just the person to introduce the two of them to each other. I looked for opportunities to get together and turned each conversation to Christ. After a few weeks, Jason told me that he didn't want to hang out any more. He told me he felt like a project, like I was using him to get a notch on my belt. I was shocked!

I was trying to do him a favor! I was trying to help him understand the nature of the universe. I was trying to introduce him to God. I felt personally insulted by his lack of gratitude and understanding.

I consulted the leaders in the student group, and they told me how to help him "over the hump" and into the Kingdom. I tried all the methods they suggested. We only met a few more times before he stopped meeting with me entirely. I wrote him off as "not wanting to hear the truth." The fact is, I don't think I ever actually heard him.

I was so intent on winning his soul that I never heard his heart. I know he was lonely and a bit scared. Even so, he chose to be alone rather than to spend time with me. I kept trying to get people to buy what I was selling, but I failed to demonstrate the love or care of the Christ that I was peddling. I had become the person with the simple answers. I had become the pushy person trying to shore up his own shaky faith by seeking new converts. I had met Christ and truly loved him, but I was still afraid to let him touch the tender places of my heart. To do so, I had to deny what was going on inside. As this denial continued, I became more disconnected from my heart and attempted to live out things that had no place in my heart. I was well on the way to becoming one of the hypocrites I hated.

I was quick to speak, quick to mouth trite platitudes and declarative certainties in the face of difficult questions. I was progressing through the steps to prove myself and become a leader among my peers. I was drinking in their respect. I was quickly accepted and repeatedly encouraged in my pursuit of leadership. Unfortunately, the process of advancement had precious little to do with my heart.

It was all about performance. How many people had I shared with? How many studies did I attend? How many groups did I lead? How many training modules did I complete? I was on the fast track to leadership but was losing my heart. I was becoming a Pharisee, as I strained out the gnat but swallowed the camel.

My inner life wasn't keeping pace with my performance of religious duties. I was able to teach and to lead while seeking to quench my soul thirst at the same toxic cisterns. I was continuing to seek out impurity in word, image, and—when possible—in the flesh. I kept up appearances, and even tried to occasionally evangelize those I went to bed with. I couldn't see the ludicrous hypocrisy of my life. I was telling people that they were hungry for something and that I had the answer, even as I sought to satisfy my hunger through them.

As I approached graduation, it began to dawn on me that I had no idea what I was going to do next. My compatriots in the student fellowship had a ready answer. Several of them were going to spend the next year overseas evangelizing those who had never heard about Jesus. Most of them were going to the Soviet Union. They invited me to come along. I protested that I had no desire or aspiration to be a missionary. They countered with the question, "What else are you going to do?" I had to admit they had a point.

They encouraged me to apply and to leave it in God's hands. That seemed like an easy way to get them off my back, so I applied. I told God that if He wanted me to go, then He would have to get me into the program. I told Him that if I got in, I would follow that path as far as it ran. I halfheartedly filled out the application. I believe that there was a question about my "calling" to the mission. I wrote that I didn't have a "call" or even a desire to go, but was just applying because I had no other plans. I sent off the application and didn't give it a second thought.

As my university days were drawing to a close, my father's health continued to deteriorate. I was finishing projects and papers, preparing for final exams, while monitoring his condition from afar. It had been more than a month since I had last visited home. I was anxious to see him, but he and my mother encouraged me to stay focused on my studies. I was finally applying myself and was enjoying learning. I was even vaguely considering graduate school. I was doing well and I wanted to finish strong, but I was also looking forward to spending the summer at home with my family.

Finally, graduation day arrived. The rebel in me didn't even want to attend the ceremony, but my family insisted. They wanted us to all share this important milestone. My mother made arrangements for some friends to stay with my father while she, my brother, my sister and her boyfriend, an aunt and uncle, and my grandparents all came to celebrate with me. The ceremony was unremarkable. It was held outside in an amphitheater, and it started to rain not long after I walked across the stage. I didn't stay for the end of the ceremony, but signaled to my family in the stands that I was leaving. We met outside the theater and made plans for lunch.

My mother and grandparents headed off to pick up lunch, while my siblings and I went back to my place. I have a vague memory of joking around with my siblings and generally having a good time that afternoon. Not long after I arrived, I received a phone call from our friend who was staying with my dad. She asked to speak to my mom, but she hadn't arrived yet. I asked if there was a message I could relay. She insisted on speaking with her directly. It was another hour before my mom came to the house. They had become lost while looking for the place to pick up lunch. She looked concerned when I told her about the call. I showed her into another room where she could call them back in private. A few minutes later, with tears spilling from her eyes, she came out to tell us that my dad had died. The time of death coincided exactly with the time I had walked across the stage to receive my degree.

We were all shocked. I was angry that we were at my graduation rather than at his bedside. It was about an hour later that people started showing up for my graduation party. A stranger celebration I cannot imagine. Many of my friends at university had never met my father or any of my family. I watched through tears as the two worlds I inhabited intermingled. In the shadow of death, we celebrated my graduation.

The next day we hastily departed for home. There were funeral preparations to make and a fatherless future to face. I returned to a home that was alien and strange. My father was no longer there. It wasn't his physical presence that was missing as much as the vacuum that was created in the relational space of the family. My brother and I found my mom asking us for input on things she would have normally discussed with my father. In this, and a thousand other small ways, it came home to us that he was gone and that our lives would forever be different.

The preparations for the funeral were all a bit of a fog. I was dimly aware of a procession of visitors, most with some sort of food in hand. I struggled to recall my last interactions with my father and to make sense of our relationship.

I had visited several times while away at university. The first few times I visited, the farewells were tearful, but over time they became more casual. I wished I'd been able to say a final goodbye. It's not that much was left unsaid. His death wasn't unexpected. We all knew it was coming, but the ending was sudden and managed to surprise us nonetheless. I thought we'd have time for at least one more talk before being cleft apart.

CHAPTER 6

THE LORD PROTECTS CHILDREN AND FOOLS

After my father died, I moved back home. University was over and my family needed me, or so I thought. It turns out they had figured out how to live without me. It's not that I didn't make contributions, but there was no need for me there. They had cared for my father and had endured the worst of the cancer struggle without me. I have heard that there is a camaraderie that is forged in a foxhole. Men who join the unit later, but who were not in the foxhole, are on the outside of this kind of bond. I felt that then. My family had lived through a battle while I was largely absent, or only occasionally present. They had changed, and so had I.

I returned from university truly arrogant. I had become puffed up with pride. I had acquired loads of knowledge and learned to wield it ruthlessly. I had honed my argumentation and debate skills in the classrooms of the university with great success. My family found those skills less than desirable around the dinner table at home. My relationship with my sister was particularly difficult at this time. In the months after I moved back into the house, she made it painfully clear that I wasn't welcome. In her eyes, I had forfeited the right to speak into the situation by not being there when times were tough.

I also struggled with anger and bitterness toward my mom. I blamed her for not knowing what she couldn't have predicted, the timing of my father's death. If I had known he was going to die, I would have been there with him. I would have held his hand and had one last conversation. I was hurting. We were all hurting. My solution was to hide behind easy answers, and I am sure my answers were trite and unhelpful. Even if they hadn't been, I was so cocky in my delivery as to make even the choicest of spiritual delicacies unpalatable. I was sure I knew the answers to life's questions and was quick to offer my wisdom and unsolicited advice.

It was in this context that the idea of visiting Europe became so appealing. I wanted to travel and see the places I had only read about. Without any particular goals before me, this seemed like a good time to go. When I was born, my grandparents invested some money for me to use for university. I had held those funds in reserve throughout my education. I managed to work my way through without tapping into the funds. With their permission, I made plans to travel around Europe. There was a family, the Freeds, who had been sent by our church to a village outside of Stuttgart.

Jack and Debbie Freed were friends of my parents. I had met them several times in the States. I contacted them about visiting and made plans to start my trip there. I also had some contacts scattered around other places. There was a Basque foreign exchange student now living in Northern Spain, a friend of a friend in Southern France and a friend from church living in Florence, Italy. I planned to travel around Europe visiting places of interest while staying with these friends along the way. I had no traveling companions. I filled my backpack with a EuroRail pass, a few books, a few clothes and an insane amount of trail mix and beef jerky, and I flew off to Germany.

The Freed family received me very graciously, particularly as it had been years since they had seen me. They welcomed me so warmly and completely that I was in no hurry to leave. I even watched their kids for a few days while they traveled to a conference. Their home became the base from which I explored the castles, forests, museums and ruins of Southern Germany. In some of the small towns, I visited memorials to the German dead from the World Wars. I was moved as I contemplated the fact that the Germans mourned their dead too.

My eyes were being opened to the broader world by experiences not available through books alone. In a Stuttgart art museum, I spent hours in front of a painting of the suffering Christ. That picture haunts me to this day. I walked the grounds of a ruined monastery, wondering at the lives of those men, devoted to prayer and creating a beautiful abbey that had now fallen to ruin. I don't know what I was looking for, but I was hungry to see the world and to experience life. I visited churches and castles. I read books and had conversations with strangers.

I once met a group of Christian university students on a train. They were on their way to a conference. I had nowhere to go and no schedule to keep, so I got off the train with them and spent the night in a youth hostel that was located in a castle. I broke bread with these brothers and sisters and enjoyed a little taste of sweet community. The next morning we parted ways after breakfast and I was on my own again.

I found myself in a train station and ducked into a bookstore. I was drawn to the magazine rack and my eyes immediately searched out the porn. I don't know how much time I spent standing there thumbing through the magazines and filling my mind with images that enticed and excited even as they enslaved me.

My life oscillated between sin and repentance, fellowship and isolation. I read Scripture and looked at porn. I sought out fellowship and knowledge while cultivating secrecy and deception. I found myself pronouncing truths but living lies. I hated myself and was disgusted by my weakness and inability to resist temptation—all the while making plans for the next failure.

The next day, I decided to explore the caverns beneath a large ruined castle on the Rhine. As I pushed deeper into the dark, dank passageways I was simultaneously terrified and exhilarated. I don't know if I had ever experienced darkness quite like that. I kept pushing forward, wondering what was around the next corner. I suddenly found myself in a spot so narrow that I could go neither forward nor backward. In those terrifying moments, I realized that no one knew where I was. I was all alone in the side of the mountain beneath tons of earth and stone. I was trapped by my own desire for adventure, my curiosity about the darkness. Eventually, I freed myself and made my way back to the fresh air. But the lessons of my brief imprisonment were wasted on me.

Even as I wavered back and forth between pursuing Christ and indulging the flesh, I continued to believe that I was God's gift to the world. I was sure I had so much to offer. I spent a couple of weeks in Northern Spain simultaneously partying with and talking about God with Spanish and Basque young people. I evangelized my friends in Southern France while ogling the topless sunbathers on the beaches by day and flipping through pornographic magazines at night. I ventured across Southern Europe on my way toward Italy. My double life became more pronounced as I bounced back and forth between sin and sanctity with remarkable ease.

I thought I was living the dream, traveling around Europe on my own. I answered to no one and was responsible for no one but myself. I could get up whenever I wanted and set my own schedule. I could sit in front of a painting for an hour or people-watch in front of the train station. I was my own man, free and alone.

As I review my journals from this time, a clear sense of deception emerges between the lines. It is as if I was playing a role even in my private journal: trying to think deep thoughts and have deep experiences, all the while avoiding the depths of my heart. I searched for truth in art, architecture, culture and theology, while avoiding the deeper truths simmering in my heart. I don't believe I deceived anyone as thoroughly as I deceived myself.

As I traveled through Spain and Italy, I was struck by the opulence and beauty of the cathedrals and the spiritual apathy of the people. The church of St. Mark in Venice was both beautiful and disturbing. The bones of St. Mark were stolen—smuggled out of Egypt centuries ago. They'd been hidden under a load of pork so as to discourage inspection by the Muslim customs officials.

The Venetians constructed a cathedral to house their ill-gotten treasure. They covered the inside of the church with gold. They decorated the outside with golden horses looted from the Christian city of Constantinople. I found myself confused and disturbed by this mix of faith and vulgarity. They proclaimed their reverence of God extravagantly, all the while sinning boldly.

There was a stark contrast between the trappings of Christian history visible around me and the modern denial of God's reality. The churches were empty husks for corn long since harvested. Few people had any interest in God, and fewer still had any real relationship with Him. I met some believing Christians along the way, but I spent most of my time living alone in my faith and wondering about it all. I was discovering that I wasn't strong enough to live my faith in isolation. I was trying … and failing magnificently. Seeking Him in the morning—only to seek solace in the arms of another before evening fell.

I was in Venice when I learned that Charlie, the friend I was planning to visit in Florence, wasn't going to be there when I arrived. Instead, he was going to be in Greece. I'd wanted to see Greece anyway, so I made plans to catch up with him in Athens. He was working as a fashion model. As I talked with him on the phone, I grew concerned. I could tell he wasn't walking with the Lord and was in need of help. I was sure that I was going to be the one to rescue him. So, on a rescue mission, I boarded a train to Greece through Yugoslavia. Charlie was in trouble, and I was going to help him. He was so lucky to have a friend like me!

It wasn't far from Venice to the border with Yugoslavia. Before long, I was hurtling through the Yugoslavian night on my way to meet my destiny. We hadn't traveled far from the border when a train conductor came by to check tickets. He rejected my EuroRail pass and flung it back at me. He informed me that my ticket was no good. At least that's what I think he said. We couldn't understand one another at all. I took pity on the poor man. I patiently explained to him in perfect English that my pass was good and showed him the dates. As he became increasingly angry at my patronizing attitude, a student from the next cabin took pity on me and intervened.

Through Esther's patient translation, I discovered my EuroRail pass wasn't good in Yugoslavia. It only covered me from Venice to the border and from the border of Greece to Athens. I would need another ticket to get across Yugoslavia. At first, I wasn't sure this was true but decided that I could trust Esther, if not the irate conductor.

I dug into my backpack and pulled out traveler's checks to buy a ticket from the conductor. Of course, he couldn't accept American Express traveler's checks. Neither could he accept my credit card. So, now I was facing an angry conductor with no money and no ticket. Esther told me he was swearing and making plans to have me put off the train at the next station—somewhere in rural Yugoslavia in the middle of the night.

At this point, Elios, the Greek porter, stepped in. It turned out that a Greek train company owned the train car, and they always had a porter on board to make sure the car wasn't stripped while traversing Yugoslavia. He encouraged me to retreat to my cabin and not come out until we reached Belgrade. The plan was that I would buy a ticket there, and that would solve the problem. The conductor didn't seem too happy, but he grudgingly approved the plan.

When we arrived in Belgrade early the next morning, Esther and I got off the train and went to the ticket window and then the money changing office. Neither one was interested in my credit card or my travelers checks. We were running out of time and options, so we hurried back to the platform, where we found nothing. Our train was gone.

We had both left all our belongings on the train with the porter and Esther's friend. I was left standing on an outdoor platform in the foggy morning light, staring slack jawed at Esther. I apologized for getting her into this mess. Just a few seconds later, we heard our names called and saw our train pulling back in at a different platform. Apparently, the train needed to be put on a different track and we hadn't missed our train after all.

We joyously boarded the train, only to face the ugly reality that I still had no ticket and no prospects of getting one. Before long, another conductor came to check everyone's tickets or, in my case, the lack thereof. Another conflict followed with another threat of being put off at the next station. The situation continued on like this throughout the day as we drew ever closer to the Greek border.

Esther got off the train at a university town in southern Yugoslavia after advising me to stay in my cabin and not get off the train until the border, no matter what. This sounded like a good idea to me. At the last stop before the border, the conductor prepared to make good on his threat to kick me off the train. He called other uniformed men to help him throw me off the train. But the porter, Elios, stepped in once more.

He went with me to the ticket office in a tiny rural train station. He bought me a ticket from there to the border. The conductor wasn't too happy about this, as he knew that I had traveled all the way from Italy, but somehow Elios prevailed and the train moved on toward the border with me on board. I thanked the Lord for His provision and remembered something my father used to say: "The Lord protects children and fools … and I ain't no child!"

God had once again come to my rescue and bailed me out of a mess of my own making. Despite my arrogance and my lack of planning, He demonstrated that His eye is ever fixed on His children. Even in my confused state, I was able to recognize His handiwork. I was grateful for His provision.

When we arrived in Athens the next morning, I bought Elios a cup of coffee, paid him back for the price of the ticket, thanked him profusely and set out to rescue my friend Charlie.

CHAPTER 7
CHOOSING THE WORLD

Charlie and I had met a couple of years before, on a trip organized by our church. We bonded as we snuck away from the group and found a place to buy beer—not an auspicious beginning to a Christian friendship. We talked about Christ but shared similar vices and insecurities. We both repented with vigor but found ourselves drawn back to wine and women. It had been a year or more since I had seen him, and I assured myself that I was different now and would be able to help him this time.

I took a taxi from the station to the hotel where he was staying. We had decided to split a room at his residential hotel to save some money. I didn't know anything about Athens beyond its ancient history. I was eager to see the sights and to see a familiar face again. I didn't have any specific plans, but wasn't expecting what I found.

The hotel was located on a hill overlooking the city. Next door was a monastery, but it would be difficult to imagine two more different worlds living side by side. The hotel was populated entirely with fashion models from all over the world. There was a dizzying array of vacuous earthly beauty living alongside a place devoted to prayer and the pursuit of God.

I was surprised and pleased to find that these beautiful people readily accepted me as one of their own. As I accompanied Charlie to casting calls, I was reprimanded by photographers and casting agents for not bringing along my own portfolio to show my work. I didn't have a photo book, but I was flattered that they assumed I was a model. I was welcomed into the world of the stars that so many people only dream of breaking into.

We had free entrance into the most exclusive clubs and never paid for anything because the club owners wanted the models to be there. Their presence lent prestige to the establishment. I couldn't believe that I was in this swirl of glamour. I quickly fell into the rhythm. We would stay out until the wee hours of the morning, rise late, go to a couple of castings and then lounge around town seeing the sights.

For the first couple of days, I tried to talk with Charlie about God, and he was eager to do so. We prayed together and discussed Scripture, and then headed to the club or to a late-night poker game. Within just a couple of days, I was aware of the danger. The women were enticing and clearly available. The drinks were free. Everything around me screamed, "Indulge!" I halfheartedly resisted at first but ignored the prompting to flee that were rising up in my heart. I recognized the temptations. It was as if this situation was tailor-made to appeal to my weaknesses and insecurities. I saw that a trap had been laid to destroy me, but I deceived myself into thinking I was strong enough to resist and that I would rescue Charlie as well.

The fall started slowly, with small compromises. When I first arrived, I refused to drink at all. On the third night, I had a beer at dinner with Charlie. *No big deal,* I lied to myself. That drink wasn't my last. Then I started to change in other ways, and my language started to deteriorate. As a teen, I used to swear constantly, but it had been years since profanity laced my casual conversation as it did in Athens. I also began flirting with the girls more boldly. They responded more and more brazenly.

As bold as I seemed on the outside, I was amazed that these cover girls were interested in me. As we passed newsstands, billboards and buses, I saw the smiling faces of my new friends drift by, their seductive stares looking back at me. I wondered if they would look at me that way in private. It wasn't long before I found out.

By the second week, I was an established member of the community. There was no distinction between my behavior and theirs. I was one of them. The friend I had come to rescue was now dating a model from Sweden. I was playing the field, flirting with any and all of the unattached models.

One night I found myself at a particularly loud club on a beach somewhere outside of Athens. Henri, an extraordinarily drunk German male model, bitterly asked me what I had that he was missing. He wondered why I was surrounded by a bevy of beautiful women. What did they see in me? In that moment, I realized the difference was Christ in me. That same evening several of the girls asked me, point blank, why I was different than the other men in our circle. I knew what they were seeing, but I wanted them to desire me more than God.

Even in my compromised position, they had seen a dim reflection of the image of God in the way I treated them. On more than one occasion different ones asked me to share my secret with them, and I refused. I knew that if I shared the hope of Christ with them, my joyride would be over. I declined. I deceived. I demurred, and in doing so stole the glory of God for myself. I twisted their hunger for the Light of the world into a hunger for me. I cheated them.

Night after night, I sought out opportunities to turn their hearts towards me. Much to my shame, I succeeded. I spent different nights with different women. It only depended on who was at the club that night or who was most responsive in the moment. I lied to myself as much as to them. I told myself that I was getting it out of my system. I was sowing my wild oats. I was having a last fling and that, after diving in this deep, I would never want this again. I fought hard against the conviction of the Spirit. I tried not to hear His warnings.

I remember one night in particular (or probably early one morning) after returning from a club, I was tossing in my bed, struggling with guilt and shame. I felt I was beyond redemption. I had spent the last couple of weeks knowingly turning my back on Christ. It wasn't that I didn't know it was wrong; it was that I knew it was wrong and I wanted it anyway. I knew my choices were directly contrary to all that I still believed to be true.

I wasn't losing my faith. I was just choosing to ignore it. I felt completely lost and prayed for the first time in a week or more. I told God that I knew He could never forgive me. No sooner had the words escaped my tortured lips than I heard God's whispered response. He quietly spoke into my soul, "There is nothing you can do that I cannot forgive."

It was so shocking, so simple and so personal. As I lay there wallowing in my misery, He met me and reassured me so deeply. But my soul was sick. My desire to sin was strong. I was so lost that even this kindness was turned against Him. I heard another voice in my mind. This voice said, "If He can forgive you today, He can forgive you tomorrow, or next week, or next month." In that moment, I believed I had bested God. I could indulge my flesh completely and He would have to forgive me for whatever I had done. He couldn't break His promises. He could never refuse to forgive me. I could have the best of both worlds. I could sin boldly and be forgiven completely.

After that, I dove even deeper into depravity. I gave myself completely to every available indulgence. I spent every night seeking out more affection and false intimacy. I used drugs and alcohol to keep the Spirit at bay. I drowned out His voice with music and clubbing. Even a motorcycle accident failed to get my attention. I turned my convalescence into yet another way to elicit sympathy and affection from the women around me.

I think somewhere in the back of my mind, I wanted to be rescued. I knew the life I was embracing in Athens wasn't real. I knew it couldn't last. But I was too weak or too wicked to extract myself from it. It was a heady thing to be in the midst of the beautiful and to be welcomed as one of them. It is impossible to imagine a better snare to drag me away from the Father. Athens was the ultimate worldly answer for all my insecurities. I was wanted. I was desired. I was respected. It was all I'd ever wanted and yet it left me more broken than I could have imagined.

At the time, I didn't understand that the Father's will is exceedingly delightful. I still believed that by following Jesus I was giving up good things, desirable things. I had decided, on one level, that the sacrifice of following Christ was worth it. But even that was wrong thinking. Following Christ is not giving up the best to settle for something less. Following Christ is giving up the cheap trinkets of this life in order to gain something much more valuable. Even though I had been following Christ for several years, I still yearned for the world. I didn't yet believe that what Christ offered me was better than what the world had to offer. When I was presented with the opportunity to choose between them, I chose the world.

The truth is that the indulgences of the world are actually pleasurable. They are enjoyable, but fleeting. They are sweet in the mouth, but sour in the stomach. They are like candy-coated poison. They promise so much, but deliver so little and leave destruction in their wake. My reckless abandonment to my own pursuit of pleasure in Athens was damaging my own soul as well as those around me. We used each other to keep the Lord at bay. My guilt was greater than that of my companions because I knew Him and denied them the opportunity to know.

I effectively avoided Him for a few days, then one morning the phone rang in a strange room and reality came crashing in.

Now, I was faced with a clear choice. I could ignore yet another invitation from the Lord and continue to live in denial and deceit, or I could respond to the wake-up call with repentance and obedience. I would like to say that it was an easy, or even an immediate, choice to follow Him. Instead, I hung up the phone, rolled over, wrapped my arms around my sin and searched for the words to keep the illicit affair on track.

I learned later that day, on another call with my mom, that I had a couple of weeks before I had to be home. I faxed my letter of intent to the mission program and spent another week continuing to indulge my flesh. I selfishly continued to reel in the affections of women around me even though I knew I was leaving. I was preparing to return to the States to embark on a mission trip—and at the same time seeking to quench the Spirit at every turn with sinful escapism.

I was in no hurry to leave Athens or to return to the States. Athens was feeding all the needy places in my soul. But like drinking salt water, I was left more thirsty and sick after every drink. Still it was difficult for me to tear myself away. I cried as the plane took off from Athens. I was leaving all that my flesh held dear for an uncertain future. I knew it was the right choice, but it was incredibly painful and difficult.

My journey to the States led through Germany. I had left most of my belongings with the Freeds, and so my route home took me back there. I plotted a course that led me through Rome and up to Stuttgart by train. Jack agreed to pick me up at the train station and to host me for a few days as I made final preparations to return to the states. I still remember the ride from the train station to Jack's house.

I threw my backpack into the side of the van and jumped into the front seat. Jack turned to me and asked, "How ya' doin'?" "Great," I responded, as casually as I could, hoping my inner turmoil was sufficiently hidden. Something in my voice or demeanor must have given me away, because he turned and fixed me with a look I'll never forget. "How are you really doing?" he asked. I felt naked … caught. Before I knew what was happening, I burst into tears. All the pain and confusion simmering inside of me boiled over in a moment.

I spent most of the next three days crying, confessing and sleeping. I was exhausted in every way. I had indulged my flesh completely, and I had gone past the end of myself. I told Jack everything, and I asked him what was next. I knew I had disqualified myself from the ministry forever. I knew there was no way back from this failure.

The thoughts bombarding my mind broke me: *I've wrecked my future. I could never be used by God because of the depth of my debauchery, because of my total and repeated rejection of Him.* I was able to accept His forgiveness on a personal level, but I couldn't imagine I would ever be a worthy vessel for His Spirit.

These thoughts came from deep within. I had heard these phrases spoken in judgment over those whose offenses paled in comparison to mine. I honestly thought I was wrecked beyond redemption. I thought I was permanently disqualified from ministry. My view of my Father's love was too small. My understanding of my brother Jesus' sacrifice was too limited. I thought, then, that man could thwart the plans of God. I thought only a pure vessel could be used as a conduit of His Spirit.

I know now that none of us is pure. I know that every man is a mixed bag, full of honorable and dishonorable thoughts and intentions. I know too that God is bigger than our sin and our wayward hearts. I know He loves and partners with us to accomplish His will. It's a tremendous pleasure to walk with God and to collaborate with Him. One of the tragedies of sin is that we miss out on the pleasure of this journey. One of the mysteries of life is that God uses the weak, the foolish and the ignoble to accomplish His will and bring Himself glory.

I didn't understand any of this then. I only knew I had failed in every imaginable way. I thought I was beyond His love, that there was no grace left for me. I poured my heart out to the Freeds, fully expecting their condemnation to mirror my own.

Jack and Debbie listened patiently. They didn't heap on condemnation. They gave me the space and the grace to grieve. They didn't offer any simple answers. They asked questions and tenderly probed my broken heart. After a couple of days, they gently asked for an invitation to speak into my life. They told me they were encouraged by my brokenness. They had seen through my façade the first time I'd stayed with them.

They had seen a young man full of himself and closed to the Spirit of God. They had clearly seen my prideful spirit, and I had been naked all along like the proverbial emperor in his "new clothes." They assured me that I was now in a much better position to be used by God than I had ever been. Before, I'd felt like God was lucky to have me on His team. Now I could hardly believe that God would condescend to call me by name. I was a living example of the prodigal son.

God met me in the form of Jack and Debbie and pulled me into His embrace. The more I confessed my unworthiness to be His child, the more they embraced me and demonstrated His love to me. They made me know I didn't have to grovel. They loved me, and in them, I found the love of God.

They also encouraged me to make amends to those I had misled, used, and discarded. I made a series of dreaded phone calls to the girls I had selfishly seduced in Athens. I tried to explain how sorry I was, that God was offering them—and me—something better than the counterfeit intimacy we had shared. I shared about His grace and mercy. I don't know how much they understood, as language was always a challenge. I'm sure they were confused. I was speaking very differently to them now than I had before. I carry deep regret to this day that I didn't respond to their pleas for the good news about God when I was with them in Athens.

After a few days with the Freeds, a strange thing started to happen. The weeping slowed to a trickle, and I started to wonder if they might be right. Was it possible that God could still love me so completely? Was it possible that I might actually be more useful to Him now after my complete and abject failure? Was it possible that my brokenness was a prelude to my usefulness rather than a disqualification from His service? Hope was being birthed in me. Hope was growing in the rarefied light of grace, love and truth.

The Freeds didn't pass over, or minimize my sin. They agreed with me that what I had done was terrible but demonstrated in word and deed that God's love and grace were bigger than my sin. They gave me an acceptance that was far superior to the false intimacy I had found in Athens. They led me to the fountain of living water. The drink I found in that fountain made the stagnating poison of the cisterns nauseating by comparison.

I had truly spent myself on things that didn't satisfy. I'd worn myself out pursuing all that the world promised would gratify the cravings of my heart. It turned out that I had deeper desires in my heart—places in my heart that cannot be satisfied with the shallow deceits of the world. The pleasures of sin are real—I know that full well—but they are wrapped in lies. They destroy your soul while giving you a spoonful of sugar to help the poison go down.

All the acceptance and "love" I'd received in Athens didn't satisfy. It didn't touch the places in my heart that longed to be filled. I had used these women, and they had used me. None of us found anything approaching genuine fulfillment in the exchange. I knew all along that the ones I deceived didn't know or love the real me. I carefully crafted an image I thought would entice. It did that too well, but the "me" that needed love remained untouched as they responded to the false self I projected.

The Freeds knew the real me, and they loved me completely. From that place, I could begin to imagine that God, who knew me even more fully, could love me even more than they. This flesh and blood demonstration of the gospel ministered to my soul.

Once again, God was taking my horrible decisions, my self-destructive behaviors, and working them together for my good. He had lifted me out of the mire and set my feet upon the rock again. A long but hopeful road stretched before me, a new path on the continuing journey. I had a new, and very personal, understanding, of the depravity of man—not as theological dogma but as personal experience. I was beginning to understand the heart of the gospel in a new way, but was unclear where this path would lead me.

CHAPTER 8

RETURN OF THE PRODIGAL

I returned from Europe to my family and my church who knew nothing of my repentance, let alone my failure. They knew I was returning from Europe to prepare for a mission trip, but they had no clue as to what I had gone through. I knew I had to be honest about my experience. How could I hide what was happening in my heart? How could they understand the slowly blooming transformation that was happening inside of me without understanding the process leading up to it? It was so difficult to share my failures with my family and friends, but fear of falling back into deception provoked me to share the news the very night I arrived home.

The room was silent as the story unfolded. I bristled under their appraising gaze. Not everyone responded with the grace I'd experienced in Germany. Surprise gave way to disbelief, and disappointment was followed by judgment. What could I say in response? They were right. I was weak. I was raised better than that. I should have known better, and I failed miserably to live up to the standards I espoused. I was clearly not a good Christian, so how could I become a missionary now? I recognized all of these statements. I'd said much the same during my days with the Freeds. In fact, I'd gone further than they had in attacking my character and worth. Nevertheless, it was hard to have those close to me look at me with such disapproval in their eyes.

But beneath all of this, a new understanding was growing in my heart. I was beginning to recognize the problems with a performance-based version of Christianity. Our behavior is certainly important, but it isn't the core of who we are. Our behavior isn't the problem. It merely expresses who we actually are. I'd spent most of my life either trying to conform to or rebel against standards of behavior, and that was all I'd ever known. I was beginning to think differently about these things, to see the holes in what I'd been taught.

Once again, I was seeing the danger of half-truths, or partial truths. I'd been taught, "You shall know the truth and the truth shall make you free." I'd been taught the importance of knowing the Scriptures and of knowing God. The problem was that the definition of "knowing" was skewed. The typical Westerner thinks of knowledge as information to be intellectually grasped. To know something is to be able to answer a question on a test, to fill in the blank. Those in the East, along with the ancient Hebrews, hold a different perspective on knowledge. Information in the head is only the first step to knowing. Real knowledge is that which takes up residence deep inside you and flows out in how you live your life.

I excelled at the acquisition of head knowledge. I was given leadership positions and received awards for my prowess at mastering information. According to my community, my theology was good, but it was still far from my heart. My choices in Europe exposed the glaring disconnect between my intellectual beliefs and my real beliefs.

Our creeds and statements of faith are of little value in discerning what we truly believe, which is made clear by the choices we make. We never act in ways that are inconsistent with what we truly believe. I was beginning to recognize the problems in the system of belief around me. I was also realizing the growing disconnect between the new me and my Christian community.

With some trepidation, I contacted the student organization about the trip. I knew I had to tell them what had happened. I had filled out a moral questionnaire as part of the application process. I'd passed it with flying colors before, but now I'd violated virtually every part of the code of conduct. I resolved to tell the truth and to take whatever came as a result. I wasn't surprised to find that the people I told, including my friends from university, were disgusted by my failure. My actions had been reprehensible and indefensible. I knew that full well. My only hope was that Jesus loved sinners, and I was certainly among the chief of those!

I had a particularly tough conversation with a friend who'd been a close mentor at university. I knew him well. We'd spent many hours together over the previous two years. He'd been a good friend, but now he was harsh and condemning. I agreed with his assessment of my character and behavior, but I bristled at his demeanor. Finally, I'd taken all I could.

I responded that I was indeed a wretched sinner. I described for him, in more detail than I had with others, the temptations I'd faced. Then I asked if he could look me in the eye and tell me, without a doubt, that he would have passed the test. I'd failed miserably and was without excuse. I was caught in the act. Now, let him without sin cast the first stone. This challenge was met by silence, but then he softened and apologized. In the end, I was allowed to enter the training and begin preparations for the trip. At this point, I wasn't even sure I wanted to go, but I felt I should keep walking down the path until God closed the door. One of the first steps was to learn how to raise financial support. We were required to have a certain number of people committed to praying for us. We were also given a specific dollar amount to raise before we could depart. These funds needed to be in an account or committed in writing. The budget was set by the organization, and the financial goals were fairly high. I went to a training session at which we were taught to put together a clear and compelling presentation about the program. They also instructed us how to make an even more compelling pitch for financial support.

They presented us with a script—a sort of schematic guide to the conversation. Start with "A." If they respond with "B," then give answer "C," If they give response "D," then answer with "E," and so forth. Everything was prepackaged and clinical. The end goal of the conversation was to look across the table, make steady eye contact and say, "You would like to support me in the amount of 'X' dollars a month, wouldn't you?"

We were instructed not to break eye contact until they answered. If they replied negatively, then we were to solicit a one-time donation as an alternative. We were also told to be sure to get the first check before we left the meeting. This was "to help them follow through on their good intentions."

I couldn't believe it. I felt they were turning the ministry into a business. I told them I wasn't going to do anything like that. I said that if God wanted me to go, then God would have to raise the funds. I was very comfortable sharing my journey and my opportunity to participate in the trip, but I was not at all comfortable using high-pressure sales tactics. I was warned about my naiveté and was told that this was the only way to be successful. I refused to agree.

I was then told that the decision was mine, but that I wouldn't be going on the trip unless I did it their way. I was getting a late start. All the other participants had started raising funds several months earlier. In short, I had to do it their way or I wouldn't be going. I responded that I was fine with that potential outcome. I insisted that God had brought me this far in the journey and that He would see it through.

I wasn't really sure I wanted to go. Back when I applied, I told God I would walk through the doors He opened. It wasn't that I was opposed to going, but I still wasn't positive that this whole missions thing was for me. I certainly didn't want to try to force any doors open. I would be faithful to do my part. I would share information with people, but I wasn't going to solicit money from anyone. If that meant I wouldn't go, then that was just fine by me.

It's probably clear by now that I have a strong rebellious streak. A friend of mine once likened me to a man who would find a brick wall and repeatedly ram his head into it. When, to everyone's surprise, the brick wall came down, the man would immediately look for another wall to start ramming. I resemble that remark. I don't know why I run toward a challenge or a conflict rather than away from it. I suspect there is some pride, perhaps mixed in with a more redeemable aspect of my personality. I don't know that it is all evil. This drive has pushed me to attempt things for God as well, but the dark side of the gift is definitely pride.

As I approached support development, I decided to strike out on my own. I'd rejected the only training I'd received. I was left to my own devices to find a way forward. I started with the missions committee at my church and sought their approval. I sat down with my mother, and we drew up a list of people she thought might be interested in hearing about the trip. I sent a letter summarizing the opportunity. The letter also referenced my ambivalence about the trip and my desire to use the support development process to discover if God wanted me to go. I followed up the letter with phone calls to see if people had any questions or input for me, or if they would like to get together to talk more.

Over the next few weeks, I had many appointments. Some were with one or two people, and others were with larger groups. I shared about the opportunity, but didn't mention the cost of the trip unless they asked. I sought to answer all their questions but never solicited any commitments or donations. Of course, most of the people were from the church and fully understood the donation-based missions model. Several had even written checks before I arrived and attempted to hand them to me at the end of the evening. This led to some very awkward moments as I steadfastly refused to accept any donations directly.

I wanted people to have time to pray and to reflect on the evening, rather than making a decision on the spot. I wanted to be sure God was sending me. I didn't want anyone to give unless God was laying it on their heart. On several occasions, I had to be very insistent about not accepting a check or cash. I didn't want people to feel they had been pressured into giving. I was trusting that if God was truly in it, then He would remind them to put the check in the mail. If it was a result of pressure or a slick sales job, then it would fade over time. Much to my surprise, all the financial support came in over a span of just a few weeks. I was quickly running out of excuses for not going on this trip.

This support raising process was another important milestone for me in my relationship with God. He was slowly drawing me toward an experiential relationship with Him. I was interacting with Him, partnering with Him. I wasn't just looking for principles that could be gleaned from the Scriptures and then applying them to my life. I was depending on the Father, talking to him about real needs and depending on Him to speak to others and make things happen in the real world. This process of raising support was a big step into an interactive relationship with Him. It was becoming clear that He really was in this.

I'd originally considered going on this trip for fairly selfish reasons. I had no concrete plans after university, and spending a year in Russia with my friends sounded fun. I'd taken a couple of courses in Russian history and wanted to peer behind the Iron Curtain. I was also eager to see the Hermitage and the other historical sites. As the support started to come in and it seemed like God was opening the doors, I began looking forward to spending a year there.

Just two days before I was to depart, I received a distressing phone call. The organization called to inform me that I wouldn't be going to St. Petersburg. Instead, I was being sent to some city I'd never heard of in the middle of Asia. It took me a few minutes to even find the place in an atlas. I'd been selected for that particular assignment because my friends who were heading up the program needed someone hardheaded and not easily discouraged. My reputation had preceded me.

My initial reaction was shock and horror. I quickly moved on to steadfast refusal. I reached for arguments against being banished to the sticks. "I raised support based on the information that I was going to St. Petersburg." "I couldn't change directions at the last minute like this." "I'd already made plans and was getting to know the St. Petersburg team, and it wouldn't be fair to them." In fact, I just didn't want to live out in the country. I wanted to be in St. Petersburg.

I felt mistreated by leadership again. I'd agreed to sign up for one thing, and now they'd pulled a "bait and switch" on me. I protested and pouted, but I had no good reason not to go wherever they sent me. They agreed to give me a couple of days to think and pray about it. We would make the final decision at orientation.

A going away dinner was scheduled with my supporters for that evening. So a few hours later, I was surrounded with friends. I presented my arguments to them and solicited their support in rejecting this change of assignments. I figured that if my supporters agreed it wasn't good, then the leaders wouldn't send me somewhere in the Asian hinterland. After talking it through, we went to prayer. We agreed that God had brought me thus far, and that He must have His own good purposes to accomplish. After spending some time praying, the general consensus emerged that I should go where the leaders thought I would do the most good.

My supporters reasoned that if the leaders felt that was the best place for me, and I had no good reason to refuse, then I should submit. Submission isn't something that has ever come easy to me. I protested that it was badly done to make this change at the last minute. My friends agreed it could have been handled better; however, it appeared to them that God was in this as well. I was at a loss. It seemed that God and my friends were conspiring against me to ship me off to nowhere. But I had no good reason not to go. So I found myself unceremoniously trundled off to Central Asia, gritting my teeth and wondering what was coming around the bend.

CHAPTER 9

A WHOLE NEW WORLD

It is funny how we often don't recognize the really significant things until we're looking at them through the rear view mirror. I desperately did not want to go to Central Asia. I didn't know any of the people on the team or anything about where we were headed. There was nothing desirable about the assignment from my perspective. Nevertheless, by the time I got to orientation, I had come to grips with the fact that I was going.

I knew my initial refusal to go was based on selfishness. It wasn't that God had told me to go to St. Petersburg; it was only that I wanted to go there. I knew if I insisted on going there, they wouldn't force me to go somewhere else. In the end, I accepted the assignment and joined a small team for one of the most amazing years of my life.

The team was composed of six single people: three men and three women. We were all pretty strong personalities, but we hit it off from the start. The team leader, Jim, was a former wrestler and football player from Texas. He used one of his two allotted bags to bring his weight lifting set. I was a little hesitant about the jock from Texas, but he turned out to be one of the most influential people in my life.

Jim was a force to be reckoned with. He was not shy about his opinions and wasn't troubled by a lot of self-doubt. Not long after we met, he made the confident assertion, "There are two kinds of people in the world: Americans and those who want to be Americans." I was dumbfounded. I was more than a little concerned about what I was getting into.

On the other hand, Jim was a very honest person with a deep love for the Lord and commitment to His Word. He wasn't afraid of the tough questions and was one of most honest thinkers I have ever known. He was a strong leader, which was good, because I would have run over anyone who wasn't as tough as he was. He was also a real servant.

He approached our team like a coach. He saw our potential and wasn't afraid to push us beyond what we thought ourselves capable of. Under his leadership, the team quickly became a tight knit, supportive community. This was good, because we were thousands of miles from the nearest support and were going to face a number of challenges.

Many of our challenges were part of living in Soviet Central Asia, but others would be of our own making. We were all Americans in our twenties who had only a week of orientation before launching out into the great unknown. We had almost no cross-cultural training and no formal biblical, theological or missions training. We had no local language, except the little I had picked up listening to some Berlitz Russian tapes. I shudder to think how ethnocentric we were. I am amazed we even made it to Central Asia.

Just catching a flight out of Moscow was almost too much for us. No one spoke English and there were no signs in English. Domodedovo airport was a confusing maze in those days, and it had none of the clean efficiency I was accustomed to in air travel. It felt like a bus station, piled with cargo and teeming with a dizzying array of people rushing everywhere.

It took us a long time to find the right section of the airport to catch our flight. Eventually, someone took pity on us and pointed us in the right direction. This was a small miracle in itself, as pity and compassion were rare in the Soviet world. We eventually ended up in a small building next to a runway. There were about a hundred other people milling about aimlessly. We piled our luggage into a heap and sprawled out across it, nervously watching the locals who all looked suspiciously criminal to us.

Suddenly, the milling masses surged into action as a window opened in one wall. To the untrained eye, the scene was total chaos. People crushed in around the window. Whoever was closest to the semi-circular hole at the bottom of the window would thrust their arms through the hole with their travel documents in hand. The woman behind the glass would roughly grab a set of documents, speak a few curt words, check something on a list and then shove the documents back through the hole.

There was no line, nothing that resembled order or civility. There was no announcement about who should approach the window or for what purpose. We watched in fascination, as people would disappear into the chaos only to emerge a few minutes later and head out the door to a plane. Jim and I joined the mob under the assumption that this was some rite of passage, a precursor to getting on the plane.

We weren't in the maelstrom long before Jim started getting agitated. He started muttering under his breath about getting pushed and the ridiculousness of the system, or lack thereof. We were still eight to ten feet from the window when an older man tried to push past Jim. I watched in dismay as Jim grabbed the man by the back of his coat nearly lifting him off his feet and dragging him back. He didn't stop until his nose was about an inch away from the startled old gentleman.

I cringed, as he loudly said, "No!" He slowly wagged his finger from side to side in front of the man's face. Jim went on to explain to the man in very loud and simple English the inappropriateness of his behavior. He made it clear that the man needed to get in line behind us. I explained to Jim, in whispered tones, that I didn't think the man understood English. He just glared at me and pointed out that the man was now behind us and that everyone was giving us a wide berth now. He was right about that! In no time at all, we had passed the trial of the scrum and were on our way out to the plane.

As we made our way toward the plane, I kept wondering when we were going to check our luggage. We never did. We walked up some steps into the baggage hold of the plane and threw our bags onto some wooden shelves. We then proceeded up through the plane where our seats were already filled by a family. We showed them our tickets and asked to see theirs, all in perfectly clear English. They just stared at us and waved us away dismissively. The argument continued for a while until nearly all the seats in the plane were filled.

We told the ladies on our team to grab whatever seats they could find, while we straightened out the problem with our own seats. That never happened. In the end, there were more passengers than seats, and so Jim and I ended up sitting on the steps leading down to the cargo hold and praying that the flight wouldn't be too rough. To top it all off, a woman sitting near me pulled corn on the cob out of her bag followed by a live chicken. I knew we were not in Kansas anymore.

We were picked up at the airport by an American we'd never met. He took us to some truly awful accommodations that had been arranged by the local university. No sooner had the girls been shown into their room when the young men from the floor above leered down at them through the hole in their ceiling. We didn't even stay the night. Jim immediately insisted that we be taken to some other accommodations. There was nothing readily available on short notice, but God made a way for us to stay at the most modern hotel in town. It wasn't the Ritz, but it was clean and without holes in the walls or floors. Unfortunately, they would only agree to a one-night stay. I suspect this compromise was only reached because the American with us spoke the local dialect.

Early the next morning, I accompanied Jim down to the lobby to arrange to stay longer. I had become the interpreter for our group. I'm sure I didn't understand even ten percent of what was being said, but

I was the interpreter! With dictionary and phrase book in hand, we tried to make our situation clear. The woman behind the desk steadfastly refused to let us stay another night. She did concede that we could leave our bags behind the desk during the day while we searched for a place to stay. At least, that is what I think she said.

We hauled our bags downstairs and went in search of new lodgings. By evening, we had found nothing. We returned to the hotel to restate our case and asked to stay another night. They agreed we could stay one more night. It went on like this for more than a month. Each morning they would "kick us out" and each evening they would let us stay for "one more night." In the meantime, we were looking for more permanent accommodations, and for people with whom we could talk about God.

What we lacked in preparation and insight, we made up for in zeal. We were eager to share Jesus with university students. Our philosophy was that university students were the future leaders and opinion shapers. By reaching them, we would have the greatest chance of long-term impact upon the nation. We spent hours hanging out on campus or going door to door in the dorms. We looked for anyone we could communicate with and seized every opportunity to make a simple presentation about Jesus.

More often than not, this consisted of a lot of pointing to Russian language editions of a tract we were familiar with, hoping they could read and understand it. Soon, we began to find students who could speak English, so we started English clubs on as many campuses as we could. We used these weekly meetings as opportunities to build relationships as we made short presentations on selected topics and then broke into discussion groups. We carefully chose topics we hoped would provide opportunities to turn the discussion toward spiritual things.

It was in these early days that I noticed a small group of rough-looking young men loitering in front of the hotel. They were black marketers selling Soviet military watches, fur hats or anything else they could get their hands on. We were warned not to talk with them or have anything to do with them as they were criminals and weren't to be trusted.

I immediately liked these guys. They spoke some English, and within the first couple of days, I started to build a rapport with them. Three days after our arrival, I shared with them about Jesus and they seemed interested. I offered to meet with them every week so they could practice their English if they would study the Bible with me. They eagerly agreed.

When I shared this new development with the team, they were much less enthusiastic than I. They reminded me that we were here to reach the leaders. If we did that effectively, then the leaders would reach the rest of their nation, criminals included. Starting a Bible study with small-time crooks seemed neither strategic nor prudent. It was simply not what we were there to do. I argued that everyone needed Jesus. In the end, I was forbidden to start the Bible study and encouraged to direct my efforts in more fruitful directions. Another lesson in submission.

The following morning I stopped on the way out of the hotel to tell my new friends that I couldn't meet with them. They were disappointed. As I shared that we had come specifically to meet with students, their faces lit up. They explained that they were students too! They were enrolled at various universities and colleges around town.

Armed with this knowledge, I hopped on a bus with my team to head to the main university. On board, I announced my plans to launch a study with my band of criminal students. The team still wasn't sure it was wise or strategic, but in the end, I was allowed to do it because they were students. I could go ahead as long as I was careful.

I started meeting with the guys several times a week at local cafés, and they also started coming to our English clubs on campus. Jim was somewhat relieved when he found they actually were students. We had wide-ranging philosophical debates and often ended up back at the question of the identity of Jesus. This merry band was composed of a Turkic Central Asian, a Ukrainian, a Russian and a Jew.

We became good friends and had a lot of fun together. The Central Asian in the group was the best English speaker. He would often serve as the translator when we got stuck. My Russian was coming along as well. I was desperate to communicate and to understand what was going on around me.

Some people learn languages from books. I'm not very good at that. Soon after we arrived, we took a couple of weeks of formal Russian at a local institute, which I found terribly frustrating. I felt I was spending most of my time listening to other foreigners repeatedly mispronounce the phrase, "Good morning."

I know this systematic approach works for many people, and I'm sure you end up with better grammar. But for me, jumping into the deep end of the pool is the best way to learn language. I'm highly motivated to swim rather than sink, and so I learned by stumbling through. I learned to speak Russian by speaking. I had no training in language acquisition at the time, but I ended up learning by what is sometimes called the "LAMP" method (Language Acquisition Made Practical). Essentially, I learned by failing repeatedly and learning from my mistakes.

It wasn't pretty, but by the end of the year, I was able to lead studies in Russian with non-English speakers. I wouldn't recommend doing it the way I did, as I made many, many mistakes. My friends took great delight in teaching me local idioms that weren't polite. They sat back watching as I used them in a Bible study or in front of their grandparents. More than once, I was scolded by the English professors at the university for speaking Russian like a criminal.

It wasn't long before our conversations outstripped our limited abilities to communicate across the language and cultural barriers. The conversations got deeper, but they sometimes slowed to a crawl as we searched for the right words. We were talking about the nature of ourselves, our souls, the universe and God. We were searching for truth together.

I'd never experienced anything quite like it. The process was so different than what I had used before. Instead of presenting simple canned answers, we were searching the Scriptures and wrestling for truth together. It was challenging and invigorating, and I was encouraged and amazed when, one by one, my new friends began to embrace Christ. Then, their friends and some of their family members began to come to Him as well.

As their parents and extended families took their first tentative steps toward belief, I was invited into their homes. I was eager to help, to serve, to guide and to teach these wonderful people. Just beneath the tough Soviet exterior, there was an abiding interest in spiritual things. They had lived through the communist inflicted spiritual famine, and now they were starting to wake up and were hungry for Truth, for God.

Again, I was running off the reservation. I was reminded that we were there to reach students, not families, not the general public. I wasn't allowed to follow up on these openings and opportunities. It wasn't part of our strategy. I felt like my hands were tied, and I again struggled to submit. I tried to find others with whom to connect these hungry people, and I even succeeded in some cases. But our strategy was to reach students and so I headed back to the campuses for ministry.

It wasn't tough to start a conversation on a university campus in those days, as we were obviously foreigners. When people learned we were Americans, it wasn't hard to draw a crowd, and there were only a handful of Americans in the heart of Soviet Central Asia in those days. We were often the first Americans people had ever met. Frequently, when we tried to transition conversations to talking about Jesus, we received blank stares, and sometimes they asked if Jesus was our boss, or the leader of our group.

I was confused by their questions, and it wasn't until I began to understand that they had never even heard the name of Jesus that their questions started to make sense. Growing up in America, I never considered the fact that there were people who had never heard the name of Jesus. In America the gospel is everywhere available, even if little understood and even less embraced. But in those days in Central Asia, there was nothing. They had no context for God, had never seen a Bible and had never heard of Jesus Christ. My eyes were being opened to a whole new world.

I knew there were people who were living without a relationship with God, or who had rejected Jesus. I had been one. But until I moved to Central Asia, it had never occurred to me that there were people who had never been given the opportunity to even hear or respond.

We shared the message of hope with thousands that year, and we had the privilege of seeing more than seventy people make a decision to follow Jesus. It was amazing to watch seeds of truth bloom and grow, seeds sown into hungry hearts by faltering hands.

It wasn't all victories and conversions. I led a number of study groups through the year, but not everyone we talked to was interested. Only one out of ten showed any interest at all. We made up for this by striking up conversations with anyone who would listen. Of those who expressed an interest, only a handful believed.

I spent a lot of time with a group made up primarily of Turkic students who were studying journalism. They were skeptics and atheists by training and education, but were Muslim by culture. We met every week for six months. In the beginning of each meeting, I presented something about Christianity and invited them to get to know Jesus. Then we spent some time reading Luke together. After a few weeks, I invited them to embrace Christ. They declined. When I asked why, they raised an objection, a question that was unanswered, a reason they couldn't believe. I offered to research their question and to discuss it with them the following week.

The next week I came back with an answer, and we would discuss it. At the end of the discussion, I asked if anything prevented them from embracing Christ. They would pose another question. Week after week, we worked through difficult questions: the trustworthiness of Scripture, the nature of truth as it relates to different cultures, the problem of evil, the paradox of knowledge and belief. They had a host of questions. Each one was posed as something that prevented them from embracing Christ.

Each week we wrestled with their previous objection until it was vanquished, only to have them raise another objection. One day at the end of the study, I asked them for their next question. They were silent.

Their eyes fixed on the floor. Finally, one of them responded that they were all out of questions. I was excited by this admission!

I eagerly asked them, "Are you ready to give your lives to Jesus, to accept Him as your Savior and Lord?"

They shook their heads sadly and responded, "No, we cannot do that."

"But why?! What prevents you? What question is unanswered?" I demanded.

"You have answered all our questions, but we cannot believe because we are Turkic. We are Muslims. Our parents, our ancestors are Muslim, and we cannot become Christians."

"But when we met you said you were atheists! If you could be atheists then certainly you could be Christians!" I objected. "Besides, if you have no further intellectual problems, no unresolved questions, and then you must believe it because it is true."

"It may be true, but still we cannot believe it. It is impossible for us."

That was the last time we met as a group. I am still heartbroken as I remember these dear friends. It has been nearly 20 years since these conversations, but I still see their faces in my mind and carry their burdens in my heart. I pray that perhaps by now they have believed. I hope they've found their way past the frontier of unbelief and into the heart of the Father who loves them.

I know He was drawing them then. I could see it in their eyes. I could hear it in their questions. There was an honest searching. At that time, they chose not to believe. That wasn't the end of their story, just the end of my part in it. The same God that drew me to Him was pursuing them as well.

Paul tells us that God uses the foolish and the weak things of the world. I certainly was well qualified by those standards. But, despite—or maybe because of —that, God used us during that year. Recently, I heard that one of my black marketer friends has become the national director of a major Christian ministry in his country. No one would have predicted that. Nearly 20 years later, we can begin to see the unfolding plan of God.

God gets all the glory for working out a strategy that only He could understand. A nation that wandered in darkness has seen a great light, even though it was brought to them in cracked pottery. He chose to partner with a headstrong and foolish young man with no wisdom or strategy to help lay the foundation for His church in a place it had never existed before. Only He knows what He is working out and why. It was an awesome experience to see God at work. What a privilege it was to get up every day, wondering what He was going to do that day. I had never been more fully alive than I was that year.

Late one night, Jim and I were on our way home after a long day of meetings and presentations. A man I knew got on the bus and sat down near the front. I wearily stood from my seat in the back and went forward. I didn't feel like sharing. I felt like sleeping. I sat down next to him and spent the next 30 minutes listening to his heart and sharing the good news that Jesus loves Him and wants to journey with him through this life. I knew God was at work in the man's heart. I felt an almost tangible sense of His presence.

After the man got off the bus, I energetically returned to my seat next to Jim at the back. I could barely contain my excitement. I turned to him and said, "Remind me some day! If I ever forget, remind me that this is what life is all about!" To be a partner with God in giving hope and life to thirsty people is an incredible privilege!

So many amazing things happened that year. All of these experiences were stretching my boundaries and forcing my mind open to new possibilities, new ways of looking at the world and understanding my place in it. As these things were happening around me, God was taking me on an inner journey that would change me profoundly.

CHAPTER 10

A NEW TRAJECTORY

My experiences in Europe stripped away many of my illusions about myself and forced me to take a long, hard look in the mirror. I had come face to face with my own weakness. I was compelled to admit I'd been playing a game, wearing masks of performance and respectability while my heart remained largely unchanged. I'd been practicing a form of godliness that was empty of power.

The form of Christianity I'd embraced wasn't working or workable. The old structure had been stripped away when it proved ineffectual, but I didn't know what to put in its place. The message of duty and obedience was inadequate to save me from temptation or even from myself. I had arrogantly "served" God, thinking I could do something for Him.

After Athens, I began to understand that the only right response to God was humble adoration and total submission. I had little idea what that meant. I had faith in God, but no framework for understanding Him or myself. My abject failure swept away my theology along with the wreckage of my pseudo-righteousness. I had nothing with which to replace it.

I was desperate for God and more than a little aware of my own propensity for self-deception. I wasn't yet free from the sins of my fathers, the traditions of my sub-culture. I had received many good things from my family and my church, but I ended up with a very warped view of God and of man. I was having a crisis of faith.

It wasn't that I was wavering in my belief in God, but I was struggling with the content of my faith. I knew God was real, that Jesus was my Savior, that the Bible was the only reliable guide; but beyond that, I was stuck. I praise God for how He reshaped my heart and set me on a new trajectory during that year in Asia.

I still haven't attained the full freedom and holiness I long for. He continues to teach me by His Spirit and through His Word. I suspect there are still many lessons yet to be learned as I travel this path. But the path is different, since both the destination and the journey have changed. I spent so much of my early years working on my behavior, but not my heart.

The traumatic failure in Europe derailed the train, but it was during my year in the heart of Asia that I found new tracks. I moved onto a new path and took a new direction. I am, even now, continuing on the journey I began that year. I'd never noticed this road before. Somehow, I had come to Jesus and joined the church, but didn't understand the depth of my need for Him. One reason I didn't see it before was that I assumed my problems would all be taken care of when I became a Christian.

Scripture tells me that when I gave my life to Christ, I became a new creation. I still believe that's true, but I previously misunderstood what that means. I thought it meant that I was totally re-made and just needed to realize what I had become. I thought the tough part was over. The change had been made, and now I just needed to work out the details in my life. This is true, but only half-true.

It's true that Jesus paid the price for my sin and removed all the barriers between God and me. It's true that to be in Christ is to be a new creation. I once was spiritually dead and now am alive; however, that is only the starting point for the new journey. I've carried a tremendous amount of baggage with me into the new life. Every part of who I am was shaped by my family, my culture and my experiences. I had developed habits of mind and body that didn't suddenly disappear that day on the mountain. I underestimated the amount of saving I needed.

I had essentially been taught that, once you were saved, it was just a matter of modifying your behavior. But what I really need is a continuing transformation. I'd been taught I was holy, and now I just needed to act like it. The reality is that I was saved and am being saved. The filling of the Spirit, the coming alive in Christ is finished. That is radical! But it isn't the end of the road, but rather the start of a new journey. I didn't understand much about this when I headed to Central Asia. I knew the old way was crumbling but didn't have any idea of what lay ahead.

Jim led us through a study that came at the perfect time for me. He created the study over the course of the year based on his reading of *Inside Out* by Larry Crabb, *Desiring God* by John Piper and the Scriptures. Jim wrote the studies each week and then led us through them. He didn't teach us as much as guide us. He asked us questions, forced us to think, and to wrestle with Scripture and the Spirit.

Each study opened with a series of questions for us to answer: true or false and why. (For example, the chief end of God is to seek His own glory: true or false and why.) We wrestled with the nature of God and man. He pushed us to examine our own foundational assumptions about God and ourselves. This came at the perfect time for me. I knew the old answers didn't work, but I didn't know where to go from there. I didn't agree with everything in either Crabb's or Piper's books, but the process of wrestling through these two books in community, with the guidance of the Spirit and the plumb line of the Scriptures, was a radically reorienting process for me.

Larry Crabb's book was written to address the question of life change. His thesis is that real change comes from the inside and makes its way outward into our behavior. Crabb writes from a Christian psychological perspective and presses the reader to recognize his or her emotions and to engage with the heart, perhaps for the first time, but certainly on a deeper level.

The Christian subculture I grew up in viewed feelings with suspicion. Emotions were unreliable at best. More often than not, they were deceptive and enfeebling. I recently heard someone from that tradition say, "In my day, we didn't worry about 'tuning our heart to God.' We just read the Word and did what it said." This is a fairly good summary of the world in which I grew up. Christians—men in particular—were strong and independent souls who always did the right thing no matter what they felt. I was taught this explicitly and had it modeled for me daily.

John Piper's book is more theological in nature. It asserts that the supremacy of God in all things is the foundation for our relationship with Him. Piper summarized his perspective this way: "God is most glorified in me when I am most satisfied in Him." God is the goal of all my desires, and all the lesser desires of my heart are like signposts pointing me toward the one great desire that underpins them all. *Desiring God* paints a picture of a completely sovereign, free and awe-inspiring God. It puts God at the very center of life and everything. It showed me not just that life change came from the heart, but that God wanted to be—had to be—at the center of my affections. My affections were not to be ignored, but instead served as indicators of the state of my heart. This ran directly contrary to what I'd been taught: that desires were bad and were to be ignored, resisted or even killed. Piper went even further to say that if we do not desire God in our heart of hearts then perhaps we're not truly converted or saved.

I now know that Scripture clearly and explicitly teaches the necessity of a change of heart for conversion. But at that time, it sounded like heresy in my ears. My alarm bells were going off. My carefully constructed walls of self-protection were being pounded down under the unrelenting assault of the Word and the Spirit. I struggled to understand these new concepts and tested them against the traditions I knew.

These new ideas sounded wrong to me. I argued hard and often, presenting the arguments of my elders. Jim patiently insisted that I search the Scriptures to see if what he was suggesting was true, rather than relying on what I'd been taught. Jim pointed out that the traditions of men weren't the issue; rather we were searching for the Truth. We wanted to know what God said, not what man taught. I couldn't argue with that.

I'd spent the last four years engaged in the vain attempt to become worthy of God's love by extinguishing my superficial sins and perfecting my performance. At times, I thought I was doing really well, but my time in Europe showed me how far from perfection I was. I'd reduced my relationship with God to sin management. I labored, prayed and asked God to help me to sin less, to purify my desires, to help me achieve the goals I set for myself. God became a means to my ends.

The point of my life had been to become more Christ-like. Christ was perfect and so I had to become perfect. Observation of my holy and happy life would then point people to God. The problem is that I'm not always happy and even more rarely am I anywhere in the vicinity of holy. So, I learned to pretend, to fake the perfection others seemed to have obtained.

Sometimes, it felt like everyone around me seemed to be doing so well. I was intimidated by their seeming perfection. As a result, I learned to wear masks that looked perfect, all the while shoring up my defenses so I wouldn't be found out to be the secret fraud I knew myself to be. I had to pretend to be perfect, to be perfectly happy and perfectly holy at all times. I had to appear to be rejoicing always and giving thanks in all things because the Bible said so. I wore the mask, even when my heart was breaking and I wanted to scream from the pain. I hid behind the façade, even when I wanted to give up and wallow in my own misery or dive in to the sinful escapes that anesthetized my soul. I tried this path and found it lacking.

Now, rejecting this superficial version of Christianity, I was re-examining Scripture to find if there was indeed something else there. I was learning to live honestly, with integrity. I like Crabb's definition of integrity: the commitment not to pretend about anything. That doesn't mean you have to share everything with everyone, but what you do share must be real and authentic. I was learning how to live from my heart.

As I was tearing down the façade and seeking to discover a new foundation for my faith, I was engaged in ministry. It was my job to tell people about God and invite them into a relationship with Him. I had to get out of the ivory tower and into the real world every day. It's odd that the words were the same as they'd always been. I could use the same tracts to share the gospel with someone, but this same gospel was now touching my heart and changing me in deep and powerful ways—ways I never thought possible. It was amazing but also scary.

I couldn't have imagined how much God would change me in one year. As I look back, I am amazed at what He did in and through me. Part of it was the way He had broken me in preparation. Part of it was living, working and learning in community. Part of it was Jim's mentoring. Part of it was the willingness to diligently wrestle with issues, without giving up. Part of it was searching the Scriptures. Part of it was the daily stepping out and seeing Him at work in circumstances, and in the lives of those around me. I saw daily evidence of His hand at work. The sum of all those parts was that God became tremendously real to me. My relationship with Him was transformed.

I'd already been teaching and mentoring others for a couple of years, but I realized now that I had been inviting people to join me on an impossible quest for perfection and finding fault with them when they fell short. I realized I'd been guilty of preaching another gospel. I had been a false teacher. James warns us that not many people should aspire to be teachers, because teachers fall under a stricter judgment. I reflected on those words with new trepidation. I knew that, in this too, I had failed. I had bound burdens onto other men's backs and hadn't lifted a finger to help them. I confessed all this and begged for God's forgiveness, which, as I was just beginning to understand, He lavished on me.

One of the most terrifying and humbling things for anyone in ministry is to teach someone what the Bible, and by extension God, says. This is a weighty responsibility. It is perhaps even more frightening, when the people you are teaching have no other source against which to check what you say. Such was the situation in which I found myself during that year.

Despite my years of wild living and my rejection of God, my childhood spent in church had filled my mind with knowledge of the Scriptures. True, I didn't rightly understand or interpret them. My eyes were being opened in that regard. But the raw data was in there. As a result, I was often called upon to teach and to lead studies. Even members of our team would seek me out to ask questions about Scripture.

Several times my friends asked me what the Bible taught about dating or some other question of particular interest to university students. I waxed eloquent about what the Bible said, and they believed me. They accepted what I said without question, because they had no reason to doubt me and no other teachers or commentaries against which to measure what I told them. I returned home at night and combed through the Scriptures to confirm that what I'd told them was actually true.

I was only too aware of how confidently I had previously taught things, which I now knew to be incomplete at best. I knew that the students I was teaching were the first fruits, the foundation for the church among a people who had never before had a church. What kind of foundation was I giving them? I was no longer confident that I was pointing them in the right direction. While they unquestioningly accepted what I taught, I didn't share their confidence in my infallibility. I knew I needed to get to know the Scriptures better, to get to know God better. I was beginning to learn how much I had to learn.

As the year was drawing to a close, I watched my teammates' anticipation grow. An eager excitement to return to the U.S. began to well up within them. Our conversations began to turn to what we would do, who we would see and what foods we were looking forward to. All the while, I had another thought in the back of my mind. I wasn't sure I wanted to go home. I found that overseas life suited me.

While I missed my family and my home in the States, it didn't seem to trouble me in the way it did others. I was raised in a fiercely patriotic home, and yet I enjoyed getting outside my own culture. I enjoyed the challenge of trying to get into the heads and hearts of my local friends, the new foods and new experiences— even learning language. I found I was pretty good at missionary life, and I derived great pleasure from it. As eager as I was to see my family and to eat a chili cheeseburger, I was going to miss life in Central Asia.

In these final weeks, I was approached about staying. Others had observed I was good at the work we were doing, and they sketched out scenarios that would allow me to stay and contribute to the ongoing work. They were concerned that if I returned to the States, I would get caught up in life there and would never return to the field. They told me cautionary tales of others they had known who showed great potential as missionaries but who never made it back to the field.

I came away from those conversations encouraged by their observations and affirmations. It was nice to know I wasn't just deluding myself, something I have quite a gift for! I began to wonder if missionary life might be what I was made for. Although I was tempted to stay, I knew that I couldn't. I had to return to the States to firm up my foundation. If I was going to preach the gospel and minister to the unreached, I had to be sure I understood the gospel and knew how to minister.

CHAPTER 11

LEARNING TO LIVE AUTHENTICALLY

One of the most difficult parts about going away is coming back. I have found I never return to the home that I left. People and circumstances change in my absence, and I change as well. This readjustment experience can be very challenging. It was hard for me to return home after university, and I'd only been a few hundred miles away. Returning home from Central Asia was a much bigger adjustment, and one for which I wasn't well prepared.

I don't know that I fully realized the extent to which I had changed on my trip. Each experience we have in life changes us in some way. We layer experiences on one another, adding new ones each day, and the more of these we share with those around us, the more connected we are. There's an argument to be made that culture itself is the accumulation of these shared experiences and the lessons we draw from them as a group.

As we interpret our experiences, we come to some agreed-upon understandings as to their importance and meaning, and we decide how these understandings should influence us as we move into the future. When I moved to Asia, I was removed from the flow of shared experience for an extended period. I was out of the stream. All the while, I was immersed in another stream and was being shaped by experiences that were foreign to my friends and family.

The process of reorienting and getting back into the flow can be embarrassing at times or even painful. We are generally unaware of the ways in which we have changed until we run afoul of some cultural norm or taboo. I was a little nervous about returning. I was at a different place, was becoming a different person. For example, I didn't even realize my dinner table manners had changed. I now ate my dinner using my fork and knife simultaneously. My mother tried to retrain me to eat in the "proper" way.

This was minor in comparison to the deeper changes. I had new understandings of God and a new commitment to authenticity. I wasn't sure how my friends and family would react to these changes. I'd initially been very resistant to the ideas I now held to be foundational truths. If they responded half as badly as I had, then I was going to be in for a rough time.

I didn't know who would be picking me up at the airport, but assumed it would be my mom or my brother. It turned out to be a larger group who made quite a ruckus in the arrival hall. I was embarrassed. I think I blushed from head to toe, but it was a great surprise. On the way out of the airport, we stopped to pick up a chili cheeseburger and then headed home for a brief party. It was such a warm, generous and loving reception. What a great beginning to my reintegration into my family and community!

Unfortunately, not everything went as smoothly as the initial reception. I participated in a few heated discussions about my new understanding of the nature of God and man. I heard from the mouths of friends and family the same protestations, the same arguments I'd used against Jim. I'd hoped my friends and family would be eager to hear about what I learned, and I believe they were; but they were also concerned that I'd gone off the deep end.

They objected that I was relying too heavily on experience and that my faith was becoming too subjective. After all, the heart was not to be trusted, it was desperately wicked. I countered that from the heart flow the issues of life. All the things we do and say come up out of our hearts. We must let God perform open-heart surgery rather than asking Him to put a bandage on our behaviors. I suspect they might have been more open to what I had to say if I'd lived out the grace I claimed to profess. I'm afraid I was drifting once more into judgment and pride, but now I was judging the judgmental and prideful.

I continued to share my newfound perspective with anyone who would listen. I was pleasantly surprised to find there were several people, even within my home church, who had arrived there ahead of me. While Crabb and Piper were the messengers God used to lead me into an understanding of the weakness of man and the grace of God, others had arrived at the same destination by other paths. At first, I found this hard to believe. My pride was such that I challenged them to clarify their positions and checked their understandings against what I'd learned.

As it became clear that we really were in the same place, I was amazed and encouraged to have companions on the journey. I'd been afraid I would be alone on this new path, but God had gone before me yet again to provide comrades along the way. As I began to relax and lose some of my defensiveness, others were able to see that I actually was changing.

Some were eager to read the books God had used to bring about the change in me, and our encouraging community continued to grow.

I got involved in student ministry again at our church and was quickly on staff and teaching in the college group. My church had a close relationship with a seminary nearby, and I started classes shortly after arriving back in the States. The next few months were extremely busy as I worked full-time in a warehouse to pay the bills, carried a full class load at the seminary and volunteered at the church. I was also loving life. I was growing in my relationship with God, studying His word and learning to live authentically in both non-Christian and Christian environments. It was a very busy season, but a blessed one.

Looking back, I'm so grateful that I was doing all three things at once. In seminary, I was learning concepts and skills I could test out in the laboratory of life. I had many opportunities to share what I was learning: formally in the church, or informally at lunch or on break in the warehouse. I learned again that the best way for me to truly master something was to teach it. If I could digest something well enough to teach it in my own words, then I had made it mine. If I couldn't explain it to one of the people in the warehouse, then I probably didn't understand it myself.

It was sometimes a strange thing to bounce from the profane environment of my workplace to the staid halls of academia and on to the sometimes-grim realities of church life. Each world was so far removed from the other, but the warehouse was probably the most authentic of the three.

The people I worked with were unabashed sinners, but they were honest. They teased me and called me "preacher boy." But as I lived among them, I noticed they would come to me when they had questions or problems. I became a sort of informal chaplain to those hurting souls. They were the bottom of the socioeconomic food chain, uneducated and crass, but they were dear people whom I believe God was particularly fond of. I know I became very fond of them.

I was amazed at their hunger for the things of the Spirit, once they discovered it was safe to talk to me. More than once, they remarked about how different I was from what they'd expected, what they'd experienced from Christians. They asked me why I was different, and this time I didn't steal any glory from God. I shared my story with them, and they responded. More than one of them professed their desire for God. Most of them didn't show the kind of changed life that demonstrated a real change of heart, but I knew how my own journey toward God was filled with fits and starts, rises and falls. My greatest encouragement during this time was a young man named John.

John was a high school dropout, and whenever he wasn't at work, and occasionally when he was, he was drunk or high. He was living with his girlfriend and had a pretty rough persona. One day he plopped down in a chair across the table from me in the lunchroom. I was trying to catch up on some studies for class and had my Bible and some theology books strewn across the table. Everyone usually gave me a pretty wide berth when I had my Bible out. John plopped down across from me and asked me what the deal was with "this whole Bible thing." That was the start of a beautiful relationship.

John had grown up Catholic but didn't attend church any more. He was pretty suspicious when he found out I wasn't Catholic. He had no idea what separated Protestants and Catholics, but he knew we were on opposite sides of something. I asked if we could set that aside and just talk about God and the parts of the Bible we held in common. He agreed this was a good idea. I suggested we start reading through the Bible, a chapter a day, and discuss it after work on Fridays. He agreed and we started in the Gospels.

John was a true seeker. He had no axe to grind, no theology to defend, and he approached Scripture with real openness and simplicity. He wasn't searching the text to find ammunition for his next theological argument, like the people at the seminary, constantly haggling over doctrines and dogmas. He wasn't mining the text for principles he could apply to make himself healthy, wealthy or wise or to use as a bludgeon in the next church business meeting. He was looking for Jesus, and he found Him there in the pages of Scripture.

I had come to believe that the Spirit of God was always previous, always at work. The Spirit is always drawing all men to the Father through the Son, and the Word of God is the best way to introduce people to Jesus. Therefore, the best way to help someone to come to faith or to grow in their faith would be to get them into the Word and to trust the Spirit to guide them to the aspect of truth that was most important for them. My studies with John gave me the perfect opportunity to test this theory.

Each Friday evening, we would get together at a local restaurant. I would ask him what he'd read and if anything had jumped out at him. He would invariably relate a story that touched him, a question or a problem he had with something in the text. I did my best to point him to the text for answers or to lead him to another portion of Scripture that would provide an explanation or a broader context in which to place the specifics. I never taught him hermeneutics. I never didactically taught him the value of context or the principle of interpreting Scripture with Scripture. I simply did it with him.

It wasn't long before he was wrestling with the identity of Jesus. He found a compelling picture of Jesus in the Gospel accounts. It was so fun for me to watch the well-worn stories shock and surprise John. I watched as the agony of the crucifixion washed over his face and as the miracle of the resurrection took hold of his emotions. One day, he asked how to follow Jesus, how to become a disciple. It was with great joy that I helped him over the threshold into the household of God.

He asked if it was OK if he didn't go to my church, but instead went to a Catholic Church in his neighborhood. I encouraged him to share with the local priest about our studies together and about his decision to follow Christ. I was encouraged, and somewhat relieved, when he returned the following week and shared about the warm embrace of the priest, as well as the priest's encouragement to continue studying with me.

The following weeks were difficult for me. John continued to live with, and sleep with, his girlfriend. He continued to drink, smoke and swear like a sailor. Everything in me wanted to rebuke him and tell him how he needed to change, that his behavior was not glorifying to God. I wanted to tell him that he was a Christian now, and he'd better start living like one. I held my tongue.

We continued to meet for study, and he continued to express his eagerness to grow closer to Jesus. I could see improvements in his demeanor, and his girlfriend remarked that he was changing a lot and for the better. But his lifestyle was far from Christ-like. I decided to continue to guide him toward the Word and the Spirit and to let the Spirit do all the convicting in His perfect timing. John was God's child, and He could raise him as He saw fit. After the Gospels, we decided to read Ephesians to give him a general understanding of the basics of the faith.

One Friday he came into the restaurant looking somber. He sat down across the table from me and asked me what "sexual immorality" meant. I asked him what he thought it meant and prayed for the Spirit to guide his answer. With tears in his eyes, he said he thought it meant that he needed to stop sleeping with his girlfriend. I agreed. He then pointed out that later in Ephesians, it said he shouldn't be getting drunk either. I agreed. I could see he was wrestling inside. He'd lived his whole life doing whatever he felt like doing, and now he was faced with submission. I knew the feeling.

I explained to John what I'd been learning: that God doesn't give us rules to keep us from good things. He gives us guidance about the best way to live, the way that will give us the closest relationship with Him and will be best for us as well. I told him that God wasn't out to rip him off, but wanted to exchange the lesser for the greater, the worse for the best. I recognized it would be a step of faith to give up what he knew for the unknown, but I encouraged him to follow through on what he felt God was saying and to see what happened as a result.

He asked why I hadn't told him these things before. I told him I wanted him to hear it directly from the Word and the Spirit, in God's timing. That way, it was an argument between him and God, rather than him and me. He smiled and agreed it was probably a wise course of action. And he chose then and there to submit to God.

We talked about the practical options for bringing his life into line with what God required of him. He decided not to sleep with his girlfriend again until they got married, and they were married a week later. John and I continued to meet as long as I worked in the warehouse and off and on for a few months after that. I watched him grow and entrusted him to the Spirit. It was such a beautiful thing to be a midwife as God birthed new life in John and then to release him to grow at God's pace.

A few months later, the church offered to hire me as the college ministries director. I would only have to work part time in order to make the same amount I was making in the warehouse. I found it difficult to leave the people at the warehouse, but I knew this was the next part of my journey. My life shifted focus, as I was no longer surrounded by non-believers. Between the seminary and the church, I was almost always among those who claimed allegiance to Christ.

I soon found myself missing the open and honest ways of my warehouse co-workers. The church had more politics and posturing than I'd seen at the warehouse—more ego too. I found it an almost constant challenge to look past words and actions and to love the hearts of people in the church. At times, it was much more difficult to stomach the biblical platitudes spoken with quiet vitriol than it had been to be surrounded by blatant profanity. But I knew that God was particularly fond of these broken people too, even if they were better at hiding their brokenness.

Church ministry gave me new opportunities to teach and to lead. I was responsible to preach twice a week, to build a staff and to lead a discipleship group. I discovered I was hopeless as an administrator and learned to value the contributions of a more diverse group of people than I had before. Being on the church staff was a unique opportunity to meet with and learn from men who had been involved in full-time ministry longer than I had been alive.

I didn't always agree with decisions that were made, ministry philosophy or theological directions, but I learned the nuts and bolts of ministry during those years. I was also able to hone my own ideas about ministry, my commitment to authenticity and depth, my desire for community and my trust in the Word and the Spirit. I continued to learn about myself as well: my ego, my woundedness, my dark side.

A few of the men on staff took an interest in me. One has become a lifelong mentor. I don't know what Bill saw in me, but he generously gave me his time, chose to invest in me and challenged me to press deeply into God. He encouraged me to explore different avenues and approaches to God, introducing me to the idea of spiritual retreats and monasteries. He encouraged me to practice solitude and silence and taught me about centering prayer and *lectio divina*. I don't think I ever left his office without a new book to read or a spiritual exercise to try.

In His infinite wisdom, the Father has pursued me through His people. God has repeatedly brought just the right person into my life at just the right time. If I'd met Bill a few years earlier, I wouldn't have been open to his guidance. I would likely have been put off by many of the things he recommended, as they didn't fit my narrow categories. But during this leg of the journey, he was the perfect companion, and he has been ever since.

Even during this time of growth and fruitfulness, I continued to struggle with lust. Since Athens, I hadn't acted upon my lust with another person. I thanked God for that degree of freedom, but I carried within me the temptations. All too often, would look for opportunities to feed the beast. Pornography wasn't as widely available then as it is today, but I found plenty of sensual images and continued to act upon these urges in private, oscillating between rationalizing my sin (the lie that no one else was getting hurt) and deep conviction and repentance.

Unfortunately, it was around this time that the Internet broke down these barriers and allowed me to search for filth in the privacy of my own home. No matter how many times I repented, I kept returning to my sin as a dog returns to eat its vomit. I memorized Scripture, prayed for strength, made commitments and developed accountability structures and relationships. I confided in, and confessed my sins to trusted friends, but try as I might, I just couldn't break free from my addiction to lust.

Most of my friends were in the "me too" category. Rather than strengthening and encouraging each other in the fight, we developed a sort of mutually assured destruction. Week after week we shared our defeats, and hope ebbed away. We shared our occasional victories as well—perhaps a few weeks of purity strung together in action, if not in thought. But even these weeks weren't real victory, because there was no real freedom. I didn't yet understand the relationship between woundedness and sin.

CHAPTER 12

A NEW LAYER OF HEALING

In the years between my surrender to Jesus on the mountain and my trip to Central Asia, I had begun to walk with God. It was a sweet time of growth, even if it left my heart largely untouched. I had been focused on the surface of my life. During this time, I began to bring many of the external sins under control. I stopped using drugs and abusing alcohol, cleaned up my foul language and tamed my lying tongue. I learned what God expected of me and tried to live accordingly.

Through this pursuit, I created the illusion of control, perfection, even holiness. I was trying to follow God on the outside, while keeping the tender places of my heart locked away. I felt the occasional tremor but had no idea what was rumbling down there. This was all taking place far beneath the surface of my life. I had learned the rules of the Christian game and seemed to be playing as well as everyone around me.

My illusions of holiness were exposed when the external controls and structures were removed. In Athens, I was away from my community and was presented with many opportunities to indulge my flesh. Left to myself, I cast off all restraint and dived right in. It wasn't that I was more holy before Athens; it was that Athens exposed the wounds that were already there.

I was disconnected from my heart. I knew I'd been wounded but had no hope for healing. I'd learned how to cope with the pain and was schooled in the art of denial. Having been taught to be tough, I learned how to walk with a limp through the journey of life. I was pretty good at it, but the Father wanted more for me than I believed was possible.

God wanted to heal me. I didn't have to live with a limp. He wanted to do surgery on my soul, to bring full healing, full restoration. He wanted me to learn to live in freedom, health and power and to live as Jesus had lived. I didn't yet know the brotherhood of Jesus. I knew His deity but had misunderstood the importance of His humanity. I knew the power of Jesus' death but didn't yet appreciate the significance of His life.

Jesus modeled for us the eternal kind of life. He was born, lived and died as a human, and He showed us what a life lived in union with the Father could be. He walked the dusty roads of this world and navigated the dingy marketplace of life with freedom, power and joy. He made it through, unstained by the world. Then He pulled back the veil and invited us to join in the dance that He, the Father and the Spirit have been dancing from eternity past.

He showed us what real faith is—not a bundle of dogmas to be believed but a relationship with a Person to be enjoyed. He moved through life with freedom and grace because He was continually connected with the Father. He grew in faith, experienced suffering and learned to trust His Father. He showed us that we could trust the Father too.

I wish someone had told me this. I suspect some tried, but I simply couldn't imagine what they meant. I thought the path I knew was the only path, that the wounds were at the core of me, that I had to live with the pain. I didn't yet know the power of the Father that raised Jesus Christ from the dead. I didn't yet understand the gift of eternal life and was unwilling or unable to trust God with the depths of my heart.

After my experience in Athens, I was broken. The Lord met me in that place of brokenness and very kindly restored me. The first step was the conviction of sin and the revelation of the wounds that still made me limp. This was the most painful part as He held up a mirror and allowed me to see myself truly. Only after I saw myself as I was did He move on to the next step.

Through my friends in Germany, He applied the healing balm of love and grace and painted a picture of hope and restoration. He helped me imagine what my life could be like in real relationship with Him. He was teaching me humility and was helping me see what was true about Him and about me. I was created to live in a love relationship with my Creator.

These were only the initial steps after the trauma. The year in Central Asia was like physical therapy for my soul, as day by day, week by week, I was pushed and prodded, both intellectually and spiritually. I used muscles I didn't even know I had, and this period of extended recovery redirected my life in ways I am still working out. Although I was learning a lot about myself, God and ministry, my worldview, so badly in need of reform, was still incomplete.

I knew I had to live authentically, that this authentic kind of life would flow from the inside out, but as I glimpsed the depths of my heart, I was afraid of what I would find. I'd spent my life trying to avoid my heart. I had underestimated the degree of healing that was required, because I had been taught a true but overly simplistic approach to life and God.

When Jesus died on the cross, He took our unholiness upon himself, exchanging His holiness for our sin. He offers to make us whole and holy. If we will accept His gift, He will make us new. I believe this is true, but there are other truths that aren't expressed in this simple explanation of the gospel.

Paul talks about an inner struggle, a wrestling within. He says that one part of him does things that are repulsive to another part of him. There is a tension between the now and the not yet, as Paul describes himself as a man torn between two realities: his new heart and his old flesh.

According to Paul, I am right now seated in the heavenly places with Christ Jesus, pure, holy and set apart for God. I have been crucified with Christ, and now He lives in and through me. I am to be holy as He is holy. But in the real world, it isn't as easy as it sounds, and it doesn't work out quite that cleanly or that simply.

I desire God, but I'm also drawn to sin. I'm thirsty for God but prone to foolishly wander off the path that leads me to Him. I'm regularly confused by my own—often competing—desires. I struggle within and often don't even know how to pray. I am holy right now because Jesus has made me so through His death and resurrection. The same power that raised him from the dead is now available for me, but I am also tempted right now by my own evil desires that come from somewhere within me. Someday, the glory of God will be revealed in the complete redemption of the sons of God, and all of creation longs for that day. I know I long for it too, but it isn't yet. I am saved and am being saved. I am holy and am becoming holy. It's the becoming part I find so frustrating.

I want to be holy now. I recognize in the biblical accounts of Jesus a man fully alive. Jesus is the second Adam, who enjoyed total freedom and unbroken intimacy with the Father. He showed us what human life was meant to be. In His life, we find the perfect model. He was whole and holy, free and happy, powerful and passionate. He was and is the perfect man, who lived a sinless life in a sinful world.

His family and friends weren't perfect, and the time and place in which he lived were far from idyllic. But He lived a real life in the real world and managed to do so with an almost unimaginable grace and freedom. He was tempted, but not compelled by the temptations; assailed, but not overcome. I love that He did it, and in Him we have all that we need for life and godliness.

I'm frustrated by my own inability to live that life. But again, I've twisted the story and made it about me. I want to live that life, to be free from compulsion, from sin. But what if the center of the story isn't about the actions Jesus did? What if He modeled a deeper truth that wasn't primarily about performance?

Jesus spoke and acted as He did because of a deeper reality as He lived in constant contact with His Father. He emptied Himself and neither spoke nor did anything apart from His Father. His life is inspiring, but when we focus on holiness or Christ-like behavior as the end, we miss the point. His relationship with the Father is the true miracle.

We were made in the image of God, to walk and talk with Him, to be partakers of the divine nature. But we exchanged that reality for the illusion of independence and control, and we chose—and daily choose—to be independent from God. Jesus showed us that true freedom is found through submission to and union with God. The freedom and power are not the point, the relationship with God is.

I wasn't free from sin because parts of my life still weren't His. I was withholding myself from Him, and I wanted to use Him for my ends rather than submitting myself and aligning my will with His. God wants me to find my satisfaction in Him, but I was continuing to run to other things—things that cannot satisfy. I was spending my time, energy and money in pursuit of the thing He longed to give me for free.

Jeremiah says it this way, "My people have committed two sins; they have forsaken me, the fountain of living water, and they have dug cisterns for themselves, broken cisterns that cannot hold water." Jesus picks up this metaphor in John 7 when He says, "Come to me all who are thirsty and drink."

I was impatient with the process. I still am. I thought freedom was the point, but freedom is a by product of an authentic relationship with God. In fact, our wounds and our weakness keep us dependent on God, which is the best place to be. The Apostle Paul had a weakness he called "a thorn in the flesh." We don't know exactly what it was, but we know he asked for God to take it away. Much to his surprise, God refused. Three times Paul asked, and each time his petition was denied. God's response is telling as he assured Paul, "My grace is sufficient for you, for my power is made perfect in your weakness."

God doesn't want us to be independent of Him, to ignore our pain and tough it out. We weren't designed for that. God wants us to belong to Him and to be with Him. In the process of walking with God, He rubs off on us and we start to look more like Him—to take on the family resemblance. Along the way, we discover that we have become free as we become more like Jesus. We become free because we live like Jesus did, in union with the Father.

In the years following my trip to Central Asia, I was in ministry and in seminary. I was growing and serving. It was a good time, but I wasn't finding freedom because I was only seeking freedom. During this time, God brought men into my life to challenge and encourage me. They pushed, prodded and invited me to pursue God. They shared their foibles and failures with me and showed me what it was like to press on after God in the real world as real men.

Each of them followed slightly different paths toward God, but I learned from them valuable lessons that helped to further develop and fill out my worldview. I learned about spiritual warfare, the value of counseling and the spiritual disciplines. I didn't choose one path. I chose them all. I dove into God's Word, prayed against the devil and his minions and changed my lifestyle to minimize, if not eliminate, temptations. I learned the value of real vulnerability and the camaraderie that comes from sharing our journey with others. I did all I could to press into the Father, and some of these lessons came more easily than others.

I grew up in a family and in a church culture that specialized in masks. I was trained at an early age not to show weakness, and some of the hard knocks I received along the way reinforced this. Once, as a teenager, I approached my parents about counseling, but my father responded that only crazy people needed counseling and that no one in our family was crazy. That brought our conversation to a quick conclusion.

It wasn't until I was in seminary that anyone I respected went to counseling. I was surprised to find that a friend of mine was going and finding it very helpful. As he described his experience, I was intrigued. My friend and I had similar struggles with lust, and I knew I hadn't found freedom on my own, so at that point, I was desperate enough to try even counseling. It didn't hurt that we had a heavily subsidized counseling program available through the seminary.

Over the next few months, I met with a counselor, sometimes more than once a week. I told him I struggled with lust and I wanted freedom. Week after week I poured out my heart, and he asked me questions. I often didn't understand how his questions were related to what I'd shared. I know it's a cliché, but it seems that much of what we discussed related to my father. My dad was not perfect, and I often protested that I didn't see the connection between my dad and my lust. My counselor never explained. I often made plans to quit counseling, but something compelled me to keep going. I don't recall much about our conversations during those times, but I remember one session.

Somehow, in the cut and thrust of our dialogue, we ended up talking about my dad again. We explored a particular episode in my teens, and I told him about a time when I'd approached my father for his opinion about some new clothes. My dad was sitting at the dining room table working on something. I asked him to look at me. He didn't respond, so I came closer. I asked him to look at what I was wearing and tell me what he thought. He made a dismissive response of some kind, without even turning around. I became a little more insistent, cajoling him, telling him I wanted him to really look at me. He spun around in his chair, with fire in his eyes, launching into a brief tirade. I don't remember all he said, but I do remember his accusation that I was acting like a girl. The sarcasm, mocking tone and biting derision cut me to the heart. I turned and silently crept back to my room.

I relayed this to my counselor in a very matter of fact way, sharing the information, devoid of emotion. I probably shrugged and laughed it off, but the counselor wasn't buying it. He suggested we try something different, something we'd never done before. He suggested a role-play. He would be my dad, and I would be me. I shrugged and agreed. He encouraged me to put myself back in that place and to tell him what I would have liked to say to my father.

I don't recall how I responded at first; I think I was pretty dismissive. I felt uncomfortable with the exercise. He poked and prodded verbally until he pushed me to tell him how I really felt. Suddenly, without warning, I exploded. I cussed him out, letting fly a stream of expletives the likes of which hadn't been heard from my lips for many years. I told him how angry I was at him and demanded to know what was so wrong about asking him to look at me. Afterwards, I was spent, and the counselor looked a little shocked and befuddled.

I continued to meet with him for a while after that. We talked about my relationship with God, about my feelings, about the stresses in my life. But mostly we talked about my dad. We never actually talked about the lust. It never came up, but over the course of those months, it slowly faded away. I was no longer compelled. I was finding freedom.

It happened so gradually that I hardly noticed. I understand the process better now. In the language of addiction, I had been self-medicating. Even though I was growing and healing, I still had pain in my soul. When things got too overwhelming, I would look for an escape. I was no longer drinking or abusing drugs, but my drugs of choice were endorphins. These naturally occurring morphine-like chemicals are produced in the body as a result of several things, sex being one of them.

I don't mean to reduce the complexity of my addiction to the level of physical addiction alone. Both the factors contributing to my internal stress and the various ways I sought to escape were complicated. What I do know is that God used counseling to lance these infected places in my soul. He opened these scarred-over wounds and let the poison out. As the healing progressed, my relationship with God progressed and a long sought freedom emerged. My circumstances hadn't changed significantly. I still had temptations and opportunities to sin, but I was no longer compelled. I was finding a new level of freedom.

My struggle with lust did not entirely vanish, and I'm not sure it will ever leave me completely. I suspect I will always have a certain weakness in this area, and I recognize the need to remain vigilant. However, I did gain a new kind of freedom through the counseling process. It wasn't comfortable or fun, but it was a key pathway for God's healing touch in my life.

I've found that, in times of stress I still feel the familiar tug to return to the cisterns of my youth. I'm still drawn to escape or to seek out respect and affirmation. However, the more time I spend satisfying my thirst in the fountain of living water, the more clearly I perceive the repellent toxicity of the cisterns. They have lost their hold on me. Their draw is diminishing over time.

The process of growth is painfully slow, and we live in a time of instant gratification. With the advent of the Internet and rapid delivery systems for goods and services, we have no patience for the pace of organic growth. We manufacture our meat by manipulating the growth cycle of cattle, pumping them full of chemicals and hormones to accelerate their growth. We genetically modify crops to get more, faster. We stamp our feet impatiently when our slightest whim is not immediately satisfied.

Our God, who will not be rushed or manipulated, meets us in the midst of this frenetic world and bids us to cease our strivings. While we're in a rush to grow, to produce, to change, He invites us to wait on Him, to draw near, to hearken unto Him. He tells us of his love for us and calls us His lover, inviting us to come away with Him. The same God who designed the organic world around us designed both our bodies and our souls. His ways are not our ways, and His timing is not like ours.

All this and more I learned through life and ministry during those years in the States. And it was also during this time that the Lord gave me a unique opportunity to test all I'd been learning. He brought Sarah into my life.

CHAPTER 13
A COMPANION FOR THE JOURNEY

I don't recall the first time I saw Sarah, but I do remember the first time I noticed her. I was home from Berkeley for the summer and helping out at the church. I went into the youth pastor's office and a blond girl with a dazzling smile was sitting there. She was filing some papers and told me that the pastor was out. Over the course of that summer, we ran into each other often around the church campus and developed a friendship.

I knew she was pretty, but I didn't think of her romantically at that time. She was 15 and I was 19. Four years is a big difference in age and experience at that stage of life. I enjoyed her company as a friend, but nothing more.

A few years later, when I returned from my year in Asia, things were different. Sarah was 19 and I was 23. The difference between us was narrowing. We started spending a lot of time together as she was one of the student leaders in the college ministry. She was also leading a Bible study group with my mother. So I saw her several times a week, either at church or in our home. Our friendship started to grow.

Up to that point, my track record with women wasn't one of purity. Since Athens, I'd been very careful to avoid dating anyone. I had a full and busy life without the complications of romance. I wasn't looking for anything, but my loving Father had other plans.

Because of our overlapping schedules and ministry commitments, we saw a lot of each other. I grew to respect and care for her deeply as a friend. Sarah had a heart for people and a listening ear. She had an attention to detail that bailed me out of many ministry mishaps of my own creation. I once planned a barbecue and forgot to bring either meat or charcoal. Only Sarah's quick thinking managed to salvage the event.

Sarah also had a passion for God. Unsatisfied to simply know about God, she wanted to know Him personally. She wouldn't be content with half measures or partial truths. She wanted to get to the bottom of things and had a quiet intensity that many missed because of her gentle spirit and her beautiful smile.

Our friendship continued to grow to the point where she was one of my best friends. I had only had one or two other women in my life with whom I had developed this kind of camaraderie. All of them had been safe relationships for one reason or another, and none of them had been single, attractive and available. Suddenly my eyes were opened, and I saw Sarah in a new way.

I was startled by the realization that there was nothing to prevent us from forming a romantic attachment. I hadn't been thinking in those categories at all and was intimidated by the prospect of changing our relationship. I was afraid of wrecking it, and I was also afraid of damaging her. Having made a hash of every previous romantic relationship, I didn't know what a God-pleasing romantic relationship looked like. This was new ground for me.

It was new ground for Sarah as well. She hadn't grown up in a stable family and had looked for love in all the wrong places. Damaged by the world, she had embraced Christ just weeks before I'd met her at the age of 15. Rather than rejoicing, there were harsh words and bitter arguments when she came to know the Father, and she faced opposition and scorn from many around her that I could only imagine.

Sarah had been through the fire. It was different than the fire I'd endured, but there was something in her that had been tempered. In her, I found not only someone whom I could love, but also someone who loved me back—someone with whom I could share my life and my passion for God.

At just the right time, God brought just the right person into my life. Sarah is a gift to me from my loving Father. She has been His hands and feet to me and has served me, showing me what humility and self-sacrifice look like. She has been His mouth to me, speaking tender words of love and encouragement. She has also spoken words I would rather not have heard. With fire in her eyes, she has confronted me when I have gone astray, when I have returned to the cisterns. Through her, I've seen more of the heart of God than I could have imagined.

As we took our first faltering steps toward courtship, none of this was clear to me. I only knew that she was the most beautiful woman I had ever seen and that she wanted to be with me. She didn't fall in love with the false me, the mask I had worn, the image I had projected. I let her see the real me. I knew our relationship had to be founded on authenticity.

God was so kind to veil my eyes as our friendship grew. If I'd considered her as a potential romantic conquest, I would have mucked the whole thing up. By the time I realized that romance was possible, she already knew who I was. She knew my family and my past, and she was one of my best friends. This was the perfect foundation upon which to build our romance.

As we grew ever closer, she saw more of my foibles. It was one thing to learn to trust God with the depths of my heart, or to tell them to a counselor. It was something else entirely to share them with a woman. To love, you must make yourself vulnerable. I had learned to make myself vulnerable to God, but had no experience doing so in a romantic love relationship.

My relationship with Sarah became the laboratory where I put into practice the things God had been teaching me. I had to keep looking to God for my identity even when there was a woman who wanted me. I had to be careful not to let Sarah, or her love, become an idol to me. I had to continue to rely on Him for the things to be found in Him alone. Sarah was my companion for the journey, but she could not be my destination.

One of the first things I ran into was my desire for respect. I had grown in this area, but it wasn't difficult for Sarah to inadvertently hurt me. I was like a field full of landmines, and Sarah was walking in the field. All of a sudden, she would find an explosion of anger as she innocently stepped to the left or the right. She didn't plant the mines in my heart, but she bore the brunt of the explosions.

One incident began as I spoke at a meeting. Sarah and her roommate were sitting in the group. At some point during my talk, I noticed that Sarah and her friend were giggling. I was immediately insecure, sure they were laughing at me. I hastily finished the talk, pulled Sarah aside and—as nonchalantly as I could—asked her what they'd been laughing about. She said it was nothing but couldn't suppress a smile at the memory.

I said nothing more that evening, but I was seething inside. I was sure they'd been mocking me. I played the scenario over and over in my head. By the time I saw her the following afternoon, I was worked into a lather. She was shocked and puzzled as I lashed out at her verbally. I demanded an explanation, but instead of waiting for her to give one, I launched into my wild accusations of disrespect. I insisted that there was no other explanation and loudly demanded an apology.

Sarah tried to explain, but I was having none of it. Finally, I grew tired of my own ranting and ran out of words. In the silence of that moment, Sarah reached out and gently touched my arm, quietly expressing her sadness at my hurt. She gingerly explained what they had actually been laughing about. It had nothing to do with me, but the enjoyment of an innocent joke with her friend had touched off a firestorm in my heart. Clearly, there was still some healing to be done in the area of respect.

Anger was a commonly expressed emotion in my family. Sadness and hurt were associated with weakness, but anger was power. It wasn't until years later that I began to understand anger as a secondary emotion, an internal response to hurt or fear. My anger that day was because Sarah had inadvertently touched one of the raw places in my heart. The mocking and disrespect I received from my father had left a wound, and when Sarah touched it, my anger was immediate.

I was like a loaded gun. Sarah touched the trigger, and the bullet was out of the smoking barrel before either of us knew what had happened. After Sarah's explanation, I felt like a heel. I apologized for my misplaced anger and thanked her for her gracious and wise response. We learned a lot about communication that day. Sarah also learned the importance of physical touch.

Our Father created physical affection to be a powerful thing. To touch another person can be such an intimate thing, and we were designed to enjoy it. It can express and complement real intimacy. When Sarah touched me that day, she reminded me that she was real and that she loved me. It brought me back to her and to our relationship. It drew me out of the past and coaxed me to look at her and to interact with her, rather than with my painful memories.

Unfortunately, physical affection can also be a counterfeit for real intimacy. There were times in our relationship when my desires took us down the road I had traveled so many times before, and lust reared its ugly head again. I praise God that he protected us from getting too far down the road before we were married, but sometimes it was a struggle. I had to resist the temptation to use Sarah to meet my own selfish desires.

God used my relationship with Sarah to press hard on my selfishness. As a single man, I was free to go anywhere at any time. I have fairly simple tastes, and God has blessed me with a very low-maintenance body. I can sleep anywhere and eat almost anything. I can even go a day or two without eating, with very little discomfort.

Imagine my astonishment when Sarah wanted to eat three meals a day. I was genuinely surprised, and rather put out, that her needs impinged on my freedom. Our relationship exposed my self-centeredness in a way I never anticipated. The exposure was good, but it was also hard for me. I imagine it was even harder for her!

Eventually, I learned how to love and serve her a bit better. I truly value and love her. She is an incredibly strong and gifted woman, and I continue to learn from her every day. As we grew into our marriage, we formed a strong and joyous partnership in life and ministry.

One of the real strengths of our relationship is how different we are. This is also one of the great challenges. It would be hard to imagine people who are more dissimilar. Over the years, we've taken many personality tests and used a lot of tools. No matter what the test is measuring, Sarah and I are always at opposite ends of the scale.

This became even more clear to us when we started premarital counseling. We'd taken some personality and values assessments to help us prepare for marriage. The counselor looked at the charts of our results and said, "If I didn't know you guys, I would say you should run for the hills! I've never seen people more opposite!" Sarah cried all the way home after that session.

We were married one semester before I graduated from seminary. We grew together and spurred one another on to love and good deeds. As we were falling in love and dreaming about our future, we were confident we would be moving overseas. We planned to return to Central Asia and were waiting for the Spirit to guide and direct. One day we received a phone call from a friend I hadn't seen in years. He was flying in from Central Asia and was eager to reconnect.

CHAPTER 14
THE PATH TO OBSCURITY

Since my return from Central Asia, I knew I wanted to move back. The more I learned about myself, ministry and missions, the stronger my desire became. Several of my mentors during that time strongly encouraged me in this direction as well. Just six months after we married, Sarah and I led a group of university students on a short trip to Central Asia. For me, it was a return to a familiar environment, but for the students and for Sarah, it was all new.

We spent a few weeks living in a village, teaching English and building relationships with local people. Despite numerous challenges, I was delighted to discover how well Sarah and I did together in this new environment. She shored up my weak places and provided insights I lacked. This was a confirmation for us that our return to the field was more than just a dream. We returned to the States and plugged into life and ministry, eagerly anticipating our future move. Another year went by, and we had a growing sense that the Spirit was moving us on. It was at this time that we received the call from a friend I'd known during my time in Central Asia.

Gordon was one of the leaders of the ministry I had gone with originally. We'd stayed in touch through the years, but it had now been nearly six years since I'd seen him face to face. In the meantime, he and his family had moved to the city in Central Asia where I had lived. He was now overseeing all the work in the country for the organization. Over breakfast, he filled us in on what had been happening since I lived there.

The ministry had progressed and grown. They were now looking to start an institute to train leaders. He described the vision and their need for someone to head up the initiative. They were specifically looking for someone with a seminary degree as well as real-world ministry experience. It soon became clear that he was recruiting me.

We were really excited! The more we thought about it and prayed about it, the more excited we became. It seemed like a role tailor-made for me among the people I loved. We sought counsel from our friends, family, mentors and pastors. Everyone agreed this was the right role at the right time. Clearly, God was opening the doors for us to return. The first step was to apply to officially rejoin the organization. That ended up being much more complicated than we'd anticipated.

While I had extensive experience in the organization, Sarah had never been involved with this particular ministry. As we went through the application process, it soon became apparent that this was going to be a problem. The application packet contained a ministry proficiency questionnaire, which scored your ability and skill in ministry. However, your score was based on your participation in and mastery of organization-specific training. Because of my previous involvement, I "scored" four and one-half out of five.

Unfortunately, Sarah, who had years of ministry experience and was very well qualified, scored only one-half of one point out of the five possible. This score caused those screening the application to wonder about the state of her eternal soul, let alone her fitness for international service. This was only the first of many hurdles we had to clear in the process. We continued to feel we were right in preparing to move to Central Asia, and already had many people praying with us to this end.

When I'd first gone out, I started the practice of a monthly prayer letter. It was a wonderful gift to have people praying for me. During my years in the States, I'd continued to send out occasional prayer letters. I figured that I still needed as much prayer as I had before. As a result, soon after our breakfast with Gordon, we had a community of people who were praying with us. This was such a gift! I've grown more and more convinced that prayer is the most important Kingdom resource we can solicit. It has been my experience that other ministry needs are taken care of when the ministry is well supported in prayer. After all, God gets all the glory for Himself when He answers the prayers of His dependent people!

The application process dragged on for weeks and then for months. At several points, it seemed to have stalled entirely. I would write to Gordon, or one of my other friends in the organization, and they would spur things along from their side. We had round after round of interviews as they tried to figure out which box we would fit into. While Sarah didn't fit well into their training boxes, I didn't fit very well into their theological grid.

In one conversation, the interviewer wanted me to commit to using a particular pamphlet, and *only* a particular pamphlet, when teaching about the Holy Spirit. I simply could not agree with that. I promised to use the Bible, and *only* the Bible, to do so. This clearly wasn't an acceptable answer. As the process dragged on, we began to wonder if we were going to like being in an organization with such rigid boxes. We wondered what God was doing.

Eleven months after we applied to join the organization, we were officially rejected. We were told, in no uncertain terms that we were not going to be allowed to go overseas. Instead, they invited us to join one of their campus ministries in the Midwest of the U.S. to be properly trained in theology and ministry. We were shocked and confused. A leader in their organization had specifically recruited us, and we felt this was God's specific invitation to return to Central Asia. We tried to appeal the decision, but there was no flexibility.

With great sadness and confusion, we wrote to Gordon about the unfortunate conclusion of the process. I was angry, confused and embarrassed. We had hundreds of people praying with us and anticipating our imminent departure. It felt like a very public failure, but it was another necessary blow to my ego. Instead of sharing the news that we were on our way, I now had to tell our friends and supporters we had been weighed in the balance and found wanting.

In answer to our letter sharing this news, I received two fateful responses. One came from a friend within the organization we had attempted to join. The head of one of their training schools in Europe and a friend from my university days, he assured me of his influence in the organization. He said that if I would just wait for a few weeks, he could straighten out the confusion, and we would be on our way.

He also assured me of my incredible giftedness and the importance of the role for which I'd been recruited. He was certain that with my gifts and talents I would excel in the role. He was sure I would be a well-known and well-respected international leader within a few years, and he told me I would soon have invitations to speak around the world and would make an incredible impact for the Kingdom.

The second letter came from a friend I had known in Central Asia. He had once been a part of the organization but wasn't any longer. His response was full of compassion for the situation we'd endured, and he invited me to come and join him in an obscure little town in Central Asia where he was working with an even more obscure little group of believers.

He invited me to join him to labor in the fields, to rely upon the Word and the Spirit to disciple these young believers and to help them become a community. He called us to come alongside this little flock and to work with them, not over them. He promised nothing except that we would work together in isolation and obscurity.

I received both of these letters on the same day. As I read the first letter, I felt vindicated, that my friend had rightly assessed my great value to the Kingdom. I was eager for his help to right the wrong I'd suffered at the hands of the bureaucrats. Everything in his letter appealed to my pride, to my flesh. I was feeling pretty good about myself until I read the second letter.

The contrast between the two was stark. No sooner had I finished reading the second letter, than my true condition was laid bare before me. I realized I had harbored secret delusions of grandeur in my heart and was falling into the old trap of thinking that God would be lucky to have me on His team. I recognized in the second letter the values I held dear. I knew, from that moment, that I was supposed to disappear into the sticks again. I knew I had to choose the path to obscurity. But oh, what a tearing there was in my soul!

Sarah came home from work that evening to find me on my face in the living room of our little apartment. Tears ran down my face as I stared at the two letters on the floor in front of me and then shared their contents with her. I disclosed my deep desire to say yes to the first one, hoping beyond hope she would provide the excuse for my disobedience. As we talked about the two options, it became clear that the second one was for us. I was in agony. I cannot tell you how difficult it was for me to stand at that fork in the road and choose obscurity.

I'd been told from childhood that I was a leader, that I had great potential. Here was an opportunity for me to show my quality, to rise to my potential, to shine. It isn't that it would have been wrong for everyone; it is a good thing to train leaders. The issue was with my heart, not with the position. It was just that it wasn't what God had for me.

Years later, I became friends with the man who took the position I rejected. While it was right and good for him, it may well have destroyed me. There was more chipping away at the stone of my heart to be done, more sculpting of my character to conform me into the likeness of Christ. With great difficulty, I set aside the first letter. I called my friend Matt, the author of the second letter, and as we dialogued over the next few weeks, it became increasingly clear that this was indeed the right way to go.

In the midst of these turbulent and confusing times, God was there. More than that, God was orchestrating it all, continuing His relentless pursuit of this thirsty fool. He was pushing on areas I thought I had dealt with, inviting me to go deeper with Him, to rely on Him more. Not content to leave our relationship where it was, He was working in and through the circumstances to draw me ever closer, opening up new vistas before me.

As we stepped forward onto this new path to Asia, the doors swung wide open. Through a series of astonishing circumstances, I ended up rooming at a conference with one of the key leaders of the organization to which Matt now belonged. As this leader and I shared our journeys and our dreams late into the night, it became clear that the heartbeat of this organization was more in keeping with the rhythm of our own.

We applied to this organization and a few weeks later were members. We prayed for God to meet our needs and shared our new ministry direction with our churches and our friends. Within four months, God provided prayer partners as well as all of our financial needs. We moved back to Central Asia just six months after receiving news of our rejection.

CHAPTER 15

TURNING POINTS

Aside from the brief visit with Sarah and the students two years earlier, seven years had passed since I'd lived in Central Asia. A visit, even a mission trip like the one we had experienced with the students, is a short-term affair. This was different. This time we weren't planning to be there for a few weeks or even a year. We'd made an open-ended commitment and were moving there for the foreseeable future. We were excited, but also somewhat fearful, about what the future would hold.

Central Asia was in transition, and many things had changed since I had lived there previously. The Soviet Union was now a thing of the past. We wouldn't be able to rely on my Russian language. I was going to have to set that aside as we together learned the Turkic language of the local people, for which there was no written grammar or dictionary. We would be forming a team with Matt and his family. We liked them, but we didn't know them well.

I was also going to have to adjust to life overseas with a wife. My expectations of overseas life sprang from my experiences as a single young man. We'd adjusted to life as a couple fairly well, but the additional stresses of all of these adjustments would push upon my selfish heart yet again.

Matt picked us up at the airport a few hours away from our new home. On the bus ride to our town, with our belongings bouncing around beneath our feet, he informed us that he would be taking us directly to live with a local family. We were surprised, as we hadn't discussed it previously. Matt was certain this was for the best, but I wasn't so sure. He dropped us off and quickly left so that we could bond with our host family. Just a few hours after arriving in country, we found ourselves staring across the table at them and wondering what would happen next.

Omirkhan was one of the leaders of the local fellowship. He'd only been a believer for a couple of years, but he was older in the faith than nearly everyone else in the church and had recently become the assistant pastor. He was one of the kindest, gentlest men I have ever known, and his wife, Aygul, was a tiny woman with a quick laugh and a deep strength that I grew to admire. We shared a two-bedroom apartment with them and their seven-year-old son, Arman.

As we sat across the table, we had only my Russian as a means of communication. We soon lost that too, as I developed a horrendous case of food poisoning and spent most of the first 24 hours in their home vomiting. My young wife tried to take care of me and to reassure the family that I wasn't dying. It was an awkward and embarrassing beginning.

In hindsight, I see the wisdom of God in stripping any last vestige of competency from me in those first few days. I was needy and dependent, and we were ignorant and helpless. We couldn't shop for ourselves, cook for ourselves, or even talk with our housemates. God humbled us before them and, upon this foundation, built a wonderful relationship. It was our first lesson in indebtedness.

As Americans, we value our independence very highly. I was raised to owe nothing to anyone. I now found myself in a situation in which I simply had to ask for help. In receiving help from others, I became indebted to them. Indebtedness felt unnatural to us, but it was a central tenet of the culture of those we had come to love and serve. Their lives were interconnected in ways we could scarcely grasp. Everyone was indebted to everyone else in one way or another. No one kept score exactly, but there was a constant give and take of mutual indebtedness that created a web of relationships and security.

Part of the arrangement of our living with them was that we would cook half the meals. This fell squarely on my wife, since local men didn't do anything in the kitchen except eat. Over the next few weeks, we realized that nearly the only time we ate meat was when we bought and cooked it. This was one of the first signs of the poverty of our new friends. We noticed that people would occasionally arrive with a big bag of rice or flour and quickly depart. We later learned that these were relatives from surrounding villages.

I still didn't realize the extent of their need until I accidently walked in on Omirkhan changing one day and saw him without his shirt on. He looked like a survivor in a photo from a concentration camp. The weather was cold, and he often had on several layers of clothing, so we'd never noticed that he was literally skin and bones.

I learned generosity from this profoundly impoverished family. They had nothing and no hope that tomorrow would be any different, but they shared generously out of whatever they had. I'd never seen that kind of generosity before. Anything I'd given was given from abundance, but they shared out of their scarcity.

We lived with this family for our first six months in the country, and it was an incredible crash course on their culture and language. We learned language relatively quickly—out of necessity—as we were immersed in the local language and culture from our first day in the country. We also attended classes at the university, where we wrestled with grammar and struggled to understand. The language of instruction was the language we were trying to learn. It was a tough and stressful time, but it was full of blessings and sweet fellowship as well.

We couldn't have asked for a better environment to motivate us to learn, or a more loving and supportive family within which to learn. The university was eager to have our tuition but was suspicious about our real reason for being there. We were pelted with constant questions from university officials, students and professors about our motivations. Why would we choose to live in this obscure little city rather than in the capital?

We were summoned by the police to be questioned more times than I can remember, and the questions came not just from the police, but from every quarter. Virtually every person with whom we spoke wanted to know why we were there, and the general consensus was that we were spies. After all, who would choose to leave one of the richest and most comfortable countries in the world to move to one of the poorest and most difficult? Who would choose isolation and obscurity when they could be where the action was?

We expected questions and opposition from the government and even the wider community, but what we didn't expect was the suspicion and opposition from within the church. We had given up everything to come and serve them, to help them. Our host family had warmly embraced us, but the reception by the rest of the leaders was decidedly cool.

Within days of our arrival, I found myself being interrogated on obscure points of theology by the local pastor. He had received a very specific, conservative and narrow theological perspective somewhere along the way. Within our first week, he invited me to participate in an exorcism (my first) and then instructed me as to why exorcisms were unnecessary. I was constantly being tried and tested, poked and prodded.

I did a little poking of my own. In one meeting, I encouraged the men to be honest with one another and to confess their sins to one another. I explained the concept of discipleship and coming alongside one another. The pastor stopped the meeting, looked me squarely in the eye and said, "That is what Americans do. We do not confess our sins to one another, and we certainly don't do discipleship! We meet on Sundays and preach the Word!"

He went on to explain why it was impractical and wrong to confess our sins to one another. He didn't seem moved by the fact that his argument flew in the face of the explicit instruction of Scripture or the modeling of Jesus and the apostles. My brief exposition of James chapter five didn't seem to help either. In the days after this meeting, I wondered why I had even come. It was clear they didn't want me there, and that I was doing no good. I decided we needed a break to get some rest and renew our perspective.

Sarah and I left for a weekend getaway at a newer hotel in the capital. We returned late Sunday night to our shared apartment. Minutes later the phone rang. It was the police insisting we report immediately to the local station. I refused to go the station at midnight, but told them I would come in the next morning. About half an hour later, there was pounding on the door. It was the police insisting that I come with them. We refused to open the door, as there had been some local robberies in which criminals would claim to be police. Once the door was open, they would stage violent home invasion robberies. We refused to open the door, and they eventually left.

Early the next morning, the police called again. They insisted I come down to the local station with passports in hand. I made arrangements to go and took Omirkhan with me. My grasp of the local language was nearly non-existent, and I wasn't confident that my Russian was good enough for this kind of situation. The police were visibly upset when we arrived. We were ushered into a back room where they began to shout and call me a criminal. After a while, it became clear that they were angry because I'd left the city without their permission.

Under Soviet law, no one could travel within the country without the permission of his or her local police. When they arrived in a new location, they had 24 hours to register with the local police. I somewhat calmly explained to them that the law they were trying to enforce no longer existed. I had researched the law carefully and had asked about it when I registered at the hotel in the capital. I knew I was right, but it didn't matter to the local police. They told me they didn't care about the national law. They were the law in this town, and they insisted I had broken it and would have to pay a huge fine.

During the interrogation, bits of information started to come out, and it became clear that they had someone watching us all the time—even to the point of having our phone tapped. They asked about specific conversations they'd overheard. I also recognized the interpreter they brought in, as we had previously seen him following us around town. Freedom and democracy were slow in coming to this corner of the old communist empire. They clearly hadn't taken the fall of the Soviet Union very well.

They were angry that their power was eroding and had decided to shake me down. It was both an expression of their fading power and a financial windfall. I was furious! It was the first time I'd been the subject of such blatant injustice, but it wouldn't be the last. I protested and argued, but there was little I could do. They held all the cards, as well as our passports, and they knew it. Despite my best efforts, I had no option but to pay. As the money changed hands, their demeanor changed as well. They were all smiles as they returned the passports and ushered us out of the station.

A friend of mine, when particularly exasperated, used to say, "It's enough to make a missionary cuss!" This saying found full expression in that moment. As we left the police station, I cursed and spat on the ground, railing against the injustice and the corruption. I decried any hope for the country and gave full vent to my anger in every available language.

As we walked home, Omirkhan remained silent as I cursed and moaned. After arriving home, my tirade continued in the living room as I told Sarah what had transpired. Eventually, I stomped off to our bedroom, threw myself on to our mattress on the floor and wept from anger and frustration. I don't know how long I lay there, but it was long enough for my mutterings to turn into prayer. I poured my heart out to the Lord, and He met me there and brought comfort. He knew what it was like to suffer under unrighteous authority. As He gently brought conviction of sin, I came to acknowledge that, although the police were wrong, that didn't excuse venting my anger on my dear host family or my wife.

A few minutes later, after I had composed myself, I was out in the living room again, this time to confess and seek forgiveness. If they were uncomfortable with my anger, they were even more uncomfortable with my confession. They were totally silent as I told them that I had wronged them by pouring out my anger on them and by cursing their country and the authorities. They squirmed as I asked for their forgiveness. They freely gave it, if only to end the awkward situation.

I didn't realize the significance of that interaction until Matt approached me a few weeks later. He said that someone in the church had just confessed to them that she had been stealing from them for some time, and asked for forgiveness. This had never happened in the years they'd been living among these people. They had suspected this person had been stealing from them, and they quickly offered her forgiveness. Then they asked how she had learned to confess and seek forgiveness.

She said they had learned it from me. She related how I'd asked for forgiveness from my host family. Aygul was so moved that she sought out a sister in the church and asked for forgiveness. Then that sister had asked for forgiveness from someone else. A wave of confession and forgiveness was sweeping through the church.

It seems that, once again, God had invited me into His plans. He took my failure and used it to teach His people. The injustice I had experienced and my angry response to it had provided a learning opportunity—both for me and for others. Jesus had come alongside me and allowed me to know what it was like to be falsely accused and suffer under unjust authorities. I wasn't suffering for my faith, but I was able to identify, in some small way, with what Jesus must have felt under the authorities in His day.

But the lesson didn't stop there. The Holy Spirit also brought conviction and spurred me on to seek forgiveness and reconciliation. God met me personally, and the ripples of that interaction spread out across the community. He was using me among these people after all. They learned more from what they saw me do than from what they heard me say.

In my failure and confession, God had brought about what I couldn't do through instruction alone. The most important part of my ministry was living honestly and humbly in community. I once heard someone say that leadership was primarily a commitment to grow in public. I have found that God uses me most in the lives of others when I am living out the things I am learning. It is true that I continue to teach and preach as He gives me opportunities, but it seems that the most powerful lessons are drawn from my life with God and my experiences of Him. I was learning that a truth has to be grasped deeply and find expression through my life before I can preach it with any authority.

After our rocky start, my relationship with the local pastor started to grow. He continued to poke and prod occasionally, but less frequently and with less animosity. One conversation in particular seemed to be a turning point. We were discussing theology, and he wanted to know if I agreed with one or another theologian and their theological system.

I responded that the theologians he was quizzing me about had been dead for hundreds of years. They had read and interpreted Scripture through the lens of their own time and culture. I encouraged him to think less in terms of adopting fully-formed theological systems and more in terms of reading Scripture for himself and interpreting it through his own cultural perspective. I affirmed the authority of Scripture and described it as the vital skeletal structure of the unchanging and unchangeable truth.

I explained that the task of each Christian is to see how these truths should be fleshed out in his or her time and place. The vital, central truths that form the backbone of our faith do not and must not change; however, much of theology isn't about these essentials but is about interpreting and systematizing. I encouraged him not to simply buy into a system created in another historical and cultural context but to cling to Scripture, trust in the Spirit and work out the Truth in a way that would be unique to his time, place and culture.

I believe he was rather puzzled by the discussion, but I also saw a light come on as he realized I wasn't trying to mold him into any particular system. I did all I could to position myself as a member of his church rather than as an authority coming from the outside to impose my theology or my culture on them. In fact, I did all I could to encourage the church to be local. The church met twice on Sundays— once in the morning for a service centered around the sermon and once in the evening when it was more open for people to share what they'd been learning.

We attended the morning service, but never led the service in any way. We felt it would be better to allow the evening service to be strictly local and therefore didn't attend. We didn't have a prominent role in any of the public services as we felt it was important for all aspects of their worship and instruction to be authentically local. We wanted it to be theirs, not ours. We did meet with the pastor and other leaders privately and encouraged them to wrestle with the Word and the Spirit to develop solutions that would be true to both their culture and to the Word, but we did everything we could to empower and encourage them to avoid dependence on us.

As we got to know one another, the pastor began to trust me and to understand that I wasn't a threat to him. One day he approached me and specifically gave me permission to meet with a young man in the church. Murat was hungry to grow, and we'd already spent some time together in various settings. He had very little formal education.

As the son of a poor family, he spent most of his formative years in the countryside watching over the flocks. Watching sheep is not particularly taxing, and he passed the time reading his culture's poets and stories. As a result, his mastery of the local language was exceptional. He was very bright and truly hungry to learn. We met at least once a week, often more frequently, whenever he would stop by.

We drank gallons of tea as we sat around our low table on cushions and shared our lives with one another. Our meetings took on a rhythm of thirds: The first third of our time together was spent sharing our questions and issues, just talking about life. We spent the second third looking at relevant Scriptures and discussing them. The last portion of our time together we spent praying.

There was no set curriculum. We discussed whatever was most on our hearts, searched the Scriptures for answers or guidance (often ending up with more questions, albeit different ones), and prayed together. I shared honestly, and I believe I got as much out of our times as he did. I often reflect on how much I learned from this brand-new believer, reading the Scriptures for the first time with fresh eyes guided by the Spirit of God.

About six months after Murat and I started meeting together, a curious thing happened. At an open sharing service on a Sunday night, he stood up and shared something he had been learning. After he was done, Murat sat down as usual. Immediately, the pastor jumped up and asked Murat where he had learned these things. Murat somewhat nervously answered that he had been meeting with me and that these were some of the things we had discussed. The pastor responded that Murat was obviously learning good things and that all the men in the church should start meeting with me every week.

What a turning point in our ministry! While it was not at all realistic or advisable for me to try to meet with all the men in the church individually, I appreciated the pastor's change of heart. I could scarcely believe it, but was certainly grateful.

Another turning point was approaching as well.

After my initial run-in with the police in our city, I made it a point to get their permission to leave the city each time I planned a trip. I was doing my best to submit to the authorities God had placed over me. I would go down to the central station and answer a bunch of questions about where we were going and why, after which they would put a stamp in my passport stating where I was permitted to travel and when.

They insisted I register in each place I visited. Upon my return, I was supposed to produce the registration stamps from the various places. This was complicated by the fact that not all local police were enforcing the old Soviet law. Each time I failed to produce a stamp, they would be upset that I hadn't received the registration from the city I'd visited. I explained what the police in the city had said about the law being out of date and no longer in force. I told them I was happy to come to them and get permission, but it wasn't within my power to make the police in other places do what they said.

One day, I returned home from a particularly unpleasant visit to the police station to find my wife in tears. I was immediately angry and wanted to know who had made her cry. I couldn't have anticipated the next words to come out of her mouth.

"I'm pregnant!" she said through her joyful tears. I could hardly believe it! Many doctors had told Sarah that she would never be able to get pregnant. She'd carried this burden for many years, but in His wisdom and mercy the Father demonstrated his tender care to us by granting us the miracle of life.

This miracle meant we would be making frequent trips to another city in the region. The women's clinic there met Western medical standards and was highly recommended for prenatal checkups. Each time an appointment approached, I had to get permission to travel.

On one such occasion, I was summarily refused. The head of the local police flung my passport at me from behind his desk and told me to leave his office. I refused, telling him either he could give me permission or I would go without his permission. He told me I couldn't do that. He had refused, and that was the end of the discussion.

I tried to calmly tell him my wife needed medical care, and I would be taking her to get it. If I couldn't go without his permission, I would sit in his office until he gave it to me. He stared at me mouth agape, then abruptly stood and came around his desk. As he approached me, he pulled back his arm and his fingers closed into a fist.

Confused by his unexpected action, I honestly didn't understand what was happening in that moment. Only later did I reflect on how dangerous the situation had been. In any event, he didn't hit me. I can only surmise that when I didn't cower, he didn't know what to do next. I stared at him, and he stared back at me for a moment with cold hatred.

Then his face softened, and his chin dropped toward his chest as he returned to his seat. He quietly informed me that he wouldn't put the permission stamp in my passport because he was wrong. I couldn't quite believe what I was hearing. Thinking perhaps I had misunderstood him, I asked for clarification. With an exasperated expression, he told me that he had no right to grant me permission to travel. The law requiring me to get permission from him was no longer in effect. I was free to travel as I liked, as long as my visa was valid. His superiors had corrected him and were forcing him to conform to national standards. I was amazed!

I returned home rejoicing and eager to share the news with Sarah. I had submitted to the authorities—never an easy thing for me to do—and God had come through for us. I had new hope for the country and for our work, but my hope was short-lived.

Just a few weeks later, I sat in the same office as he explained some complications that prevented him from renewing our visas. At first, it sounded simple: I had to get a letter from the university. When I returned with the letter, he asked for a letter from the labor department. When I got that, he asked for another letter from a different government department. Each time I got what he wanted, but each document took time and was met with a new request for further documentation. Trying to get our visas renewed became a full-time job.

I spent hour after hour in government offices trying to get the documents the police demanded. The university did all they could to help, but eventually they gave up and told us that we were on our own. It was so bad that the translator from the university asked me why the police disliked us so much. I didn't know how to respond.

We had come to be a blessing to the nation. We were taking classes and doing legitimate work at the university. It wasn't illegal to be a Christian or to attend church, and we had kept a low profile and steadfastly refused any up-front role in the church that would have caused problems. As the process continued, I gradually realized they were using the system to find an excuse to get rid of us.

I oscillated between anger at the authorities and hope that some avenue of appeal would occur to me. I prayed that God would move their hearts. I knew that the heart of kings is like water in the hands of the Lord; He turns them in any course He desires. So I figured the police would be no problem for Him, and I tried every angle.

I still remember my last trip to the police station. I can see the policeman's face as he told us that our time was up and we needed to leave. He looked like the cat that had just swallowed the canary. With barely contained glee, he expressed his regret that we had been unable to get all our documents together in time to avert this outcome. We knew this was the likely result of the process, but it was still very hard to take. We packed a few bags, made arrangements for local friends to take over our apartment and left.

CHAPTER 16

PRESSING ON MY SELFISHNESS

Almost exactly a year after our departure for Central Asia, we were back in the States. We had been planning to return to the U.S. for the birth of our first child, but we didn't anticipate the accelerated departure provided by the local police. Nor did we anticipate the uncertainty of our future. We expected to spend years working alongside the local fellowship in that small city; instead, we were denied permission to live there.

Within just a few short weeks of our departure, the other members of our team were also expelled. When the last of our team was making a final appeal to the head of the police in our town, he was told, "It does not matter what you do, what document you produce or who you talk to. We know who you are, and we will never give you visas. You and your friends will never live here."

Faced with that kind of statement, we no longer had any hope of returning to our home and our friends. We didn't feel like we were finished in Central Asia, but neither did we have any clarity about our next steps. As the baby continued to grow in Sarah's womb, we wondered what God had in store for us. Our church in the States provided a vehicle for us to drive, and a friend of the family provided a place for us to stay as we prepared for the baby's arrival and the transition to parenthood.

I used this waiting period to investigate options for our return to Central Asia. Within a few weeks, we'd secured an invitation to join another team with our organization in the capital city. A few weeks after that, we had arranged for visas. With that sorted out, we settled into our temporary situation in the States to wait for the birth.

I've known many people who look beyond their situation and stage of life with supreme confidence that their happiness lies in some other, future state. Some teenagers are sure that all will be well when they can just move out and get away from their parents. Most students are sure they'll be happy when they get a job in the real world and can escape the drudgery of classes, homework and exams. Many single people are sure that marriage is their key to bliss. I know married people who are sure their lives will be complete and fulfilled when they become parents, or parents who are sure they'll finally be happy when they can get the kids out of the house and be free again. I've never been like that. God seems to have created me with the ability to enjoy each stage of life as it comes. I've generally been happy in each season and not looked too far beyond the horizon. It's been my experience that each stage brings certain advantages and joy, but that each stage has its own troubles and less desirable experiences as well.

I believe there are real strengths to the approach that comes so naturally to me. For example, I don't spend much time worrying about tomorrow, but on the other hand, I am rarely as prepared for tomorrow as those who have spent more time anticipating it. I generally assume that life will work out, or God will work it out. I suppose this orientation, too, was a gift from my parents and the stable home in which they raised me.

As parenting approached, I had no idea what to expect. I had worked with youth and even lived with a family for a year as an *au pair* while working my way through university. While these were valuable experiences from which I learned valuable lessons, I had never had a baby. I wasn't fearful, but I also had no clue as to how it would work.

Looking back now, I can hardly believe how little I understood. In the first week after we brought our baby girl home from the hospital, I actually suggested to my wife that we run out to a movie while the baby was sleeping between feedings! Once she understood that I hadn't been joking, my wife realized she was in deep trouble with me as a parenting partner. I had a lot to learn.

God was pressing on my selfishness again. At each successive stage of my life (marriage, pregnancy and then parenting), God was revealing my selfishness. Sarah is a strong and capable person. We have a good partnership, and while the pregnancy wasn't an extremely difficult one, neither was it easy. There were some complications and a lot of nausea, and she wasn't able to continue all her work around the house or in ministry.

I felt God again chiseling away at the selfish places in my heart. He was also pushing me to be more sensitive and compassionate, traits that were never among my strong points. In fact, I have such a proclivity for insensitivity that my brother once gave me the affectionate and ironic nickname of "Captain Sensitive."

To be truly insensitive is to not sense things others might normally pick up on. I tried to explain to my wife in the early days of our marriage that I was not intentionally missing things or hurting her feelings on purpose. I really was that insensitive. I was not trying to be insensitive or merely acting as if I was insensitive. The problem was that I truly was insensitive, and therefore I needed her help.

I wasn't just making excuses. I wanted to love her well, but I recognized I would need to be more perceptive to do so. I asked her to help me by pointing out (in an appropriate time and place) things I had missed or things I could do better. She was somewhat incredulous at first. She was also fearful that I would reject her suggestions.

I can't say I've always responded well to her attempts to help. Sometimes I respond defensively at first, or she picks a bad time or place to point something out. What I can say is that inviting her to speak into my life has been the single most important human element propelling my growth. I can't imagine who I would be if not for Sarah's willingness to lovingly encourage and confront me when necessary. Her help has been essential to my growth and development as a child of God, as a minister, as a husband and as a father.

As we prepared for the arrival of our first child, we read a number of books on parenting from a wide range of perspectives and started to form our own ideas. I came to the realization that my biggest responsibility as a father is to demonstrate to my children the heart and character of God. This will lay a foundation in their hearts, and as they grow up, they will be able to more readily and rightly understand Him.

Our time in the States was pretty uneventful, but it gave us another opportunity to experience the blessings of community. We served, but were more often served by the community. They rallied around us as we waited, providing what we needed and loving us well.

After the birth of our daughter, we returned to Central Asia and started over again in a new city. We were warmly received by a new team, which also contained some friends from our old team. Thankfully, we didn't have to learn another language. Within just a few months of our arrival, we were getting settled into a new home and were able to retrieve most of our belongings from the city where we previously lived.

We also discovered we were able to maintain some, if not all of the relationships we'd formed there. While we weren't able to travel there, several of our friends traveled to meet with us. We soon had an informal network of relationships with local friends and several leaders of different churches, and out of this came two great opportunities. One was to collaborate with a local friend to see a new house church planted by and for local people. What a privilege it was to care for, counsel and support my Christian brother as he created a new community of faith among those who hadn't previously heard the name of Christ.

The other opportunity was to be involved in leadership development. I was invited to teach in two schools. Ironically, one of them was the very school I'd been invited to lead a couple of years earlier. As I got involved in these leadership development programs, I grew increasingly uncomfortable with the institutional model for leadership development. I'd seen and experienced the benefits of discipleship and leadership development in community. These institutional programs were content oriented and centered on academics. The more I read in Scripture and saw in the real world, the more convinced I was that people needed to wrestle with the issues of life in community, developing their own answers to their own questions in dialogue with the Word and the Spirit.

I agreed to teach at the school if I could design and facilitate a course encouraging the local people to identify their own issues, questions and concerns. As they identified the issues, we explored them together, in community. We would invite the Spirit to guide us to solutions through the Scriptures. I had one additional caveat: I was going to encourage the students to go out, plant churches and develop their own leaders—without sending them back to the institution for training. My fear was that the institutions would become the gatekeepers for leadership development. I saw this happening already and was hoping to be able to arrest, from within, this dangerous trend. Much to my surprise, the leaders of one of the schools agreed to my demands and I started teaching.

I also got involved in a variety of networks for leaders in the country. I was invited by my local friends to attend their meetings and also participated in those organized by foreigners. This was a busy but fulfilling season of our lives. Murat and other men from our previous town visited frequently, as did some of the women Sarah had been working with. We were involved in a local fellowship, teaching local leaders, ministering with a team, and we had a rich network of friends and colleagues among the foreign community. We were encouraged and we were growing. Life seemed just about perfect.

One day, a nurse on our team asked Sarah how she was feeling. Sarah was a little confused by the question and the evident concern on the face of her friend. She confessed to feeling tired but explained that it was probably because she was just recovering from the flu. The nurse acknowledged this, but then proceeded to quiz her about her health in more detail. As she did, a pattern emerged that we hadn't noticed. Sarah had been consistently ill for approximately four months. We protested that this was the result of an extremely cold winter and a dangerous flu season, but our friend encouraged us to see a doctor she knew. As our friend wasn't prone to be alarmist, we scheduled an appointment.

From the moment we walked in the door to the doctor's office, we could tell he was concerned. As he walked Sarah through a medical questionnaire, his concerns only grew more grave and concrete. I don't believe we'd been in the office more than half an hour when he told us he was fairly certain that Sarah had Chronic Fatigue Syndrome (CFS). He surmised that it had likely been initially triggered by a virus. This was the first time we had heard of CFS, and we didn't like what we heard.

CFS is a syndrome rather than a disease, and the diagnosis is based on the symptoms and not the cause, which remains unknown. The diagnosis can only be made by eliminating all other possible diseases or medical conditions that could produce similar symptoms. This is further complicated by the fact that the symptoms can vary somewhat from person to person.

In Sarah's case, the symptoms were chronic tiredness (which we had attributed to our busy lifestyle, rigors and stresses of living in a foreign and impoverished country and chasing around our growing daughter), cyclical flu like symptoms (which we thought had been repeated bouts of the flu) and a general malaise and heaviness (which we hadn't previously identified). He told us there was no cure and some people never recover.

This was not a good diagnosis, but on the other hand, the doctor admitted he could be wrong and that a number of diseases had to be excluded (such as Lupus and several forms of cancer) before CFS could be diagnosed. Since the other options were a life-threatening autoimmune disorder and cancer, suddenly CFS didn't sound quite as bad. Over the course of the next two weeks, the doctor ran every test he could, given the facilities available. In the end, he was able to rule out everything except CFS and pancreatic cancer. He was fairly certain that it was CFS but urged us to return to the States immediately for more testing.

I couldn't believe it. We'd already been removed from one place and were finally hitting our stride in another, only to leave. I know this was remarkably selfish and shortsighted thinking on my part, but it actually was part of our discussion. Sarah and I talked about the things we were involved in and the opportunities we had for ministry. This wasn't a good time to leave. We were firm believers in community and had often relied on the community to help us make wise decisions; so, we submitted our plans to the input of others. We decided to invite our closest friends, family, counselors and pastors to speak into the process. We laid out the medical facts and made a strong case for remaining in Central Asia. We reasoned that the prognosis with CFS was the same no matter where we were living, and so we should remain where we were.

Imagine our surprise when not just one or two, but every single person from whom we invited input, insisted we return to the States immediately for a more thorough diagnosis and possible treatment. We were torn. Obviously, we wanted Sarah to get the care she needed, but we couldn't understand what God was doing. We were frustrated and upset but felt we needed to submit. This was yet another difficult lesson in submission for me. So, less than three weeks after our first visit to the doctor, we got on a plane and left Central Asia again.

We arrived back in the States to a flurry of medical appointments. A friend had arranged for us to see a specialist within days of our arrival. This specialist ran every conceivable test, from various kinds of poisoning to obscure communicable diseases, from autoimmune disorders to cancer. It all came back negative. The only thing they could point to was some antibodies they had found in the blood that indicated Sarah had previously been infected with a couple of different viral strains which had been linked to CFS.

It was difficult to accept the definitive diagnosis confirming that Sarah was suffering from CFS. There were a couple of treatments that had been marginally effective in some cases. We tried everything, but after a couple of months, we had exhausted all the treatment options. Nothing worked, and we were left with the prognosis of chronic fatigue and suffering for the foreseeable future. The only prescription left was rest.

Our plans and dreams were gone. Our work was gone. Our commitments to the team and to the people of Central Asia were worthless and moot. I had no idea what God was doing, and I felt like He was stripping everything away—not just the bad things, but the good as well. We had no home, no car, no job and no future. I felt hopeless.

I hadn't realized, until it was gone, how much of my identity I'd taken from my work and my role as a missionary. In Central Asia, I had discovered what I was made to do, but now I was prevented from doing it. It was a bitter pill to swallow. I now spent all my time caring for my wife, sick in bed, and my increasingly active little girl—with no relief in sight.

Then one day, I received an email from an old friend of the family, Bob, who had also been a personal mentor of mine. He said he'd been praying for us a lot and suggested that we talk. He intimated that some of the things he wanted to talk with us about might blow our categories a bit. He wasn't wrong.

CHAPTER 17

THE ETERNAL KIND OF LIFE

Sarah's symptoms had continued to progress to the point where she could do nothing but lie still in a darkened room. Ironically, one of the symptoms of CFS is insomnia, and her trouble sleeping only deepened her fatigue. As a result of her worsening symptoms, she was unable to even talk on the phone, and I took the call from Bob alone.

He shared with me that a few years earlier he had begun to receive pictures in his mind's eye. The pictures had been coming with increasing frequency and clarity over the last couple of years. By the time of our conversation, he was familiar with the process and had seen some pictures that related to Sarah. He did not claim that all the pictures were 100 percent from God, but he was confident that God was behind and in them.

Bob had come to accept that he was receiving these images, but I was not there yet. It was all new to me, and I must have sounded a bit dubious. He didn't take it personally, admitting that he would be skeptical too if he were in my situation. Then, he patiently related his experiences with God and with the pictures over the previous few years and shared his process with me. He told me when and how it had started and some of the things that had happened along the way.

It was all pretty wild for me. It definitely didn't fit the categories I had been raised to adhere to. However, I had seen and experienced many things in my life and relationship with God that didn't fit the old categories. I would say that I was open but skeptical. I asked a lot of questions. We had an open and honest talk about it all, and one of the things that helped me feel more comfortable was his humility.

Most of us have run across people in our lives who claim to speak for God. This has generally not been a positive experience for me, as many of the people I've met who were most ready to speak authoritatively for God showed the least evidence of the Father's love and character—and certainly didn't emulate Christ's humility. In Bob, I saw a very different picture. He never claimed divine authority, never said he saw visions from God, never prefaced the things he saw with, "Thus saith the Lord!" In fact, he was always careful to avoid language filled with spiritual implications.

He never talked about visions, but did describe what he saw as pictures rather than using spiritual labels. He never sought to create dependency on him but always pointed us back to God. I can still hear him saying that even if the pictures were 98 percent God, there was bound to be at least two percent of Bob mixed in. He never told self-aggrandizing stories, and refused to interpret the pictures for us or to tell us what we should do.

He insisted that we take the information in the pictures to God and ask Him what to do with it. He felt strongly that the pictures were an invitation to begin a dialogue with God, rather than the end of a revelatory process. He encouraged us to seek God, to learn to discern the ways God might want to speak to us. For us, it might not be through pictures. God has a variety of means at His disposal, and we shouldn't limit ourselves to only the experiences others have had. Instead, we should seek God expectantly, waiting for Him to reveal Himself to us.

I'd been raised to believe that God spoke only through the Scriptures. While I had since learned that wasn't the case, my personal experiences with God were still quite limited. I'd learned to trace His hand at work in circumstances around me, to recognize when He was at work. I had sometimes felt His presence in worship and had a few experiences of His personal touch in times of crisis. However, I still thought of personal interactions with God as the arena of ancient prophets, rather than something that might be available to normal Christians in my day and age. God was definitely stretching my categories through Bob.

God couldn't have chosen a better messenger for us than Bob. I'd known him for years and had grown up with his kids. When I was a teenager, he'd invited me to meet with him weekly. I balked at the idea, as I was running hard and fast from everything in the church at that time in my life. Years later, after I returned to the Lord, Bob again made himself available to me. As we met together week after week, he unveiled his heart to me and allowed me to truly journey with him.

I knew Bob, warts and all. I'd seen him weep with his love for God and confess his failures and sin. I'd seen him love others and me so many times and so well. He was one of the dear ones who loved my family through my father's fight with cancer. He was one of the key men who showed me what it meant to walk with Jesus. There were few people in the world who knew me as well as Bob—perhaps even fewer whom I trusted in the way I trusted him. So, when he shared with me the pictures he was seeing, I was predisposed to trust him, even if I was a bit skeptical.

Bob started by sharing a picture of me and another man praying over Sarah in a particular manner, and in a particular place. I stood in our apartment, looking around in wonder as he told me what he'd seen. He couldn't have known it, but the place he described was the living room of the apartment we'd just moved into. He described the architectural features as well as the furniture in the room. I said nothing as he continued to describe other aspects of the picture.

He said that as we prayed over Sarah, a malevolent being, which had been tormenting her for years, was forced to dislodge and remove himself from her back. He referred to this creature as "the shaking one" and described it as having its hands sunken into Sarah's back around her upper spine. His understanding was that we were supposed to do the thing revealed in the vision and that the outcome would be Sarah's healing. He didn't know what kind of healing (spiritual, physical or both) or exactly what would be the result. However, he felt strongly that his responsibility was to relate the picture to us and to encourage us to pray. We were to seek the Spirit's guidance, and if led by Him, to actually do the things contained in the picture.

All of this was a stretch for me, and more than a little weird. I had no problem with the idea of the devil or with spiritual warfare as a theological possibility. The idea that there was some sort of evil being afflicting my wife was scary, and I wasn't sure how to deal with it. I was more than a little concerned about how to talk to my wife about all this. She didn't know Bob as I did. I wasn't certain how she would respond to the idea of a demon, or some such creature, being involved in what was happening to her body.

Much to my surprise, Sarah responded very well and was eager to figure out the way forward. We found that when we took small steps of obedience in what we could understand, the pictures would change and more information would come to light. Soon, we were able to figure out who the other man in the original picture was. It was our team leader from Central Asia, who happened to be back in the States at the time. We called and told him the story. He wasn't sure about any of this, and it was definitely outside of his boxes. But he decided there was no harm in praying about it and seeing how, or if, the Lord would confirm it to him.

Bob also received pictures of things from Sarah's distant past, things having to do with her current affliction. I didn't even know Sarah at that point in her life and had no way of verifying these things. As I talked with Sarah about these new pictures, she was able to verify them with some of her family members. We felt like God was leading us step by step, speaking very personally to Sarah's heart and expressing his tender care for her through these revelations. He had seen her, known her and loved her long before she'd reached out for Him. These sweet confirmations of His love and personal concern worked deep healing in Sarah's heart, but her body remained as afflicted as ever.

We were waiting for our team leader to get back to us, eager for him to come pray for Sarah in the manner Bob had seen in the picture. I called him again and offered to pay for his plane ticket. He was hesitant, as he'd never been involved in anything like this before. He didn't want us to waste our money, and I think he was also more than a little afraid that we would try all of this and it would fail. I was afraid of that too but had a growing confidence that God was up to something. A few days later, he called us back and said he'd just purchased tickets to come the following week. We were excited and eager for his arrival.

That evening, as Sarah and I sat down to eat, our perfunctory pre-dinner prayer stretched out into worship and adoration as we thanked God for His work in and around us. We thanked Him for speaking into our lives and for the faith of our friends. We thanked him for His provision and for sustaining us through this dark and difficult time. We proclaimed our trust in Him, no matter what the future held for us. It was a moving time. Then we ate dinner as we talked about the events of the day. Just as we were finishing dinner, the phone rang.

It was Bob calling. When I answered the phone, he asked how Sarah was. I said she was fine, and he said, "I know this is going to sound weird, but I think God just healed Sarah. I was praying for her about 15 minutes ago, and when I saw her, the being wasn't attached to her any more. I think God just healed her. What were you doing 15 minutes ago?"

I told him we'd been eating dinner but that nothing spectacular had taken place. He said he'd just received a new picture. In this one, the beings that had been attacking her were about 100 feet away and didn't seem to be able to get at her. The one that had been attached to her back was gone. He said that God's message for us was something like, "I will provide. I have not fought earnestly for you, but now I will fight for you. I am your protector. I will provide. I have something for you to do."

I sat there, looking at Sarah, a few feet away from me, searching her face or body for some sign this miracle had taken place. She looked the same to me. I thanked Bob for the call and hung up, thinking he had really missed the mark. I was ready for Sarah to be healed, but this new development didn't seem to fit with all that had been happening. I related what Bob had said to Sarah. She was hopeful, but I was skeptical.

We didn't know quite what to make of it. Our prayers that night hadn't been for her healing or even for her, in particular. We were hoping she would be healed, but we weren't expecting anything to happen until the next week when our team leader was due to visit. We were a little confused as we went to bed that night.

Around midnight, Sarah woke me up because she was very afraid and felt she was under tremendous spiritual attack. I laid hands on her and prayed for her, and she prayed too. Eventually, she was able to get back to sleep. She didn't get a lot of sleep that night, but woke up feeling rested the next morning and had a ton of energy that day. When she woke up energized after not getting a good night's sleep, we were encouraged, but I cautioned her to take it easy. Sarah had a good day, much better than she'd seen since the beginning of the illness.

The next morning, Sarah woke up feeling great and went to the chiropractor. He said she looked great and was better than he had ever seen her. He'd just seen her on the previous Wednesday, and she had horrible gland problems. He was impressed with the dramatic improvement between Wednesday and Friday. Sarah had a great time with God that afternoon and was moved to the point of tears, overwhelmed with thankfulness.

On Saturday, Sarah woke up bounding with energy, and we went to the beach. We played with our little girl and ran around on the beach for six hours. Sobs burst forth as I watched her run down the beach after our daughter—running for the first time in eight months! I couldn't believe how much energy she had! Her other mental and physical symptoms had completely vanished. I just kept telling her how excited I was to have my wife back! By then, it was starting to sink in that she actually had been healed. My skepticism was melting away in the light of the evidence staring me in the face.

Prior to her healing, Sarah had a maximum of three hours of energy per day. If she was on her feet for more than a total of two or three hours in a day, she would crash and be totally wiped out for the next few days. In fact, the two days before her healing had been crash days for Sarah. She was only up and about for an hour each day and spent the remainder of the day in bed or on the couch. Although her healing might not seem dramatic to those who hadn't lived with her and seen her crash days, it was quite dramatic for those who had witnessed it firsthand. Sarah also had a number of other mental symptoms such as the inability to read or focus. These cleared up as rapidly as the fatigue did.

On Sunday, Sarah still wasn't crashing, and we were amazed at what had transpired and so excited to worship. It was a tough day for us emotionally and spiritually as we were coming off a week of seeing and experiencing God. We attended two different churches that morning to visit with friends and to share our joy with them. Then, that evening we went to a dinner party at someone's house—something we hadn't been able to do for some time. It was another testimony of God's healing hand that Sarah still didn't crash from all the activity, but particularly because it was an emotionally tough day. We were eager to rejoice; but instead of rejoicing with us, we faced cynicism and doubt in the church.

I was surprised how disbelieving our friends were. They'd seen her before, and now a different person—a whole and healed person—stood before them. They refused to believe she had been healed. It was hard to see those who had loved us well, prayed for us and provided for us fail to glorify God or even acknowledge that He'd answered their prayers. They cautioned us to keep taking medicine and following the doctor's orders. The fact that we didn't have medicine or orders from the doctor didn't seem to faze them.

They simply patted me on the arm and said they would keep praying for us. It was ironic that Sarah's brother-in-law, who wasn't a believer at the time, was the first to suggest it might be a miracle. I wasn't very comfortable with the word, but I couldn't deny that the word "miracle" described what had happened. The children of God refused to acknowledge His handiwork, but this non-believer could recognize the truth of what had happened, even as he continued in disbelief as to the source behind it.

Our team leader still came the following week. We had a great time with him and spent a lot of time together praying and worshipping. We also prayed over Sarah in the manner that Bob had seen in his initial pictures. The first time we did so, Sarah started to weep as she was prayed for, explaining later that she was simply overwhelmed with an almost tangible sense of God's love. As we continued to act out the visions Bob had received, we never saw anything particularly spectacular. I'm not sure exactly what we were looking for, but from that time Sarah's nightmares and other dark spiritual episodes seemed to fade away.

The fruit of all this was a huge leap forward in our relationship with God, as individuals and as a couple. We continued to experience various manifestations of spiritual warfare, but we were learning how to operate in this arena with growing confidence. We felt as if a veil had been removed, and we were now seeing the world as it really is. We began to realize that God is actually everywhere, actively involved in everything.

God had been patiently pursuing me. He had been quietly wooing me. This episode felt like He was throwing open the doors and letting out a whoop of triumph. He was inserting Himself into our lives in a bold and undeniable way, and we were in awe. Through this experience, He birthed a new hope in me, and I saw, in a new way, that there was so much more available than I had dared to hope. Ironically, this experiential realization came through the consciousness that we have a real and active enemy. We'd experienced the active opposition of Satan and his demonic host; but through that opposition, God had deepened our relationship with Him. I felt like I had lived in a supernatural world with my eyes clamped shut to keep out a significant part of reality. My attempts to shut it out didn't make it less real. We started to reexamine Scripture with our eyes, minds and hearts open. As we did, we saw many things we'd missed before.

The accounts of the life Christ took on a new vibrancy, as we dared to dream that such a life might be available to us. No longer simply historical records, now they were alive with meaning. Our lives were filled with potential. Elizabeth Browning wrote, "Earth is crammed with heaven, and every common bush is on fire with God; but only he who sees takes off his shoes; the rest sit around it and pluck blackberries." We were finally taking off our shoes. We were learning what the eternal kind of life could be.

As we searched the Scripture anew, we found many references to spiritual warfare and miraculous manifestations of God. From that time on, we've lived our lives in a more integrated way. We want to live as Jesus did, in tune with the Father and not ignorant of the devil's schemes. We want all that God wants for us, and we don't want to settle into another comfortable place and stop following hard after Him. We didn't know where it would all lead, but we knew we had to follow hard after God. We knew He had intervened in our lives to bring healing to Sarah and glory to Himself and that we had to tell the story so that He would get the glory He deserved. We also knew that we were headed back to Central Asia.

CHAPTER 18

LEARNING TO DISCERN

As soon as Sarah's healing started to sink in, we began preparing for our return to Central Asia. She'd been healed almost exactly three months after we'd left our home and friends there. We were certain God had healed her so quickly and miraculously in order for us to return to Central Asia. We were eager to continue our work and were excited to rejoice in person with our team and our local friends who'd been praying for us.

We were now living with a greater awareness of God and of the enemy. We were trying to live with more awareness of the subtle movements in our desires, our minds and our bodies. As we did so, we experienced more of God in our daily lives. We were beginning to experience what Dallas Willard calls a "conversational relationship with God." Our relationship with Him and our relationship with one another were deepening. It was a sweet time, but mixed in with this sweetness, we sensed some troubling currents.

I'd been taught that God couldn't or wouldn't speak today. I now knew this to be wrong. God is still speaking to the world and to His children. God is not mute. He wants to speak to us, and He says this repeatedly in the Scriptures. He showed me this through my life and laid it bare for the world to see when He healed Sarah. Now that my eyes were open to the possibility of hearing from God, I needed to learn how to do so.

Not every thought or inner voice is the Holy Spirit, and not every strong desire is from Him. I had to learn how to tell the difference between the voices vying for my attention. There are at least three sources for these inner voices: God, the devil and myself. I've found that people often confuse these three voices, taking any inner urge and labeling it as coming from God. Others, afraid of this kind of mislabeling, refuse to listen to any inner voices. Now that I understood that He was speaking, I needed to learn to discern His voice from among the others.

For me, learning to discern the voice of God was like learning a language. It's a lot of work, but with practice, you get better at it. The

Scriptures were my textbook. In them we have a book that records the voice of God through the centuries. By reading it, we can learn His tone of voice as we see and hear how He speaks with men and women. We can become familiar with His grammar, His dialect. It's also the unchanging standard against which we can measure the things we think we are hearing from God.

The Scriptures also tell us that we have an enemy who masquerades as an angel of light. He is the father of lies. When he lies, he speaks his native language. The enemy doesn't play fair, he isn't above pretending and he's very familiar with humanity. He's been watching, and hating us, since the beginning. Through Sarah's healing, I'd seen his activity. I was aware that he, too, could speak. I'm not alone in the world with God and people. There are also enemies prowling around, looking for someone to deceive and devour.

There are still other voices in my head and my heart—my internalized scripts, ways of thinking about myself and the world. I learned these from my family, my culture and my experiences in the laboratory of life. These voices can be urgent and insistent. They have the ring of truth about them, but they're not necessarily true and are not to be confused with the voice of God.

It's too easy to oversimplify discernment. I would like to be able to share the three easy steps to discernment or give you ten keys for perfectly discriminating between these voices. But discerning the voice of God is something you learn by doing. God designed it this way because He is all about intimacy in relationship. Growth in discernment is growth in relationship. This is one way He draws us to Himself.

One important aspect of our training is to know the Scriptures, which are our safeguard. By knowing the Scriptures and testing everything we hear against them, we can eliminate much of what we might think is the voice of God. But there are many times when a situation is unclear.

Not everything is a moral certainty. There are things that are not necessarily absolutely right or absolutely wrong. When something isn't outside of God's good and perfect will, not outside of the bounds of Scripture, how do we judge it? I have a friend who once thought God was telling him to stick his finger in another man's ear and pray for him. Although it's a strange request, it isn't unbiblical. In Scripture, we find God asking His friends to do lots of strange things. How do you tell if that is God?

My friend decided to step out and see if it really was God. He approached a stranger and asked if he would mind if he stuck his finger in his ear. The stranger was surprised by the request but allowed him to do it. My friend didn't know this man was deaf in one ear. When my friend prayed, the man's hearing was restored—healed in that moment. The healing would not have taken place had my friend not responded to God. He had to hear from God and then step out and see what would happen.

Part of our training in discernment is to step out and test what we think we are hearing from God. The more we step out, the more we learn. We won't always be successful in discerning what God is saying. In any relationship, miscommunication is possible. How many times have you misheard something from a friend? You thought you heard him clearly. You thought you understood her meaning. Only as you responded did you discover you had misunderstood. We learn from our mistakes as well as our successes. It has been my experience that God usually leads us in small ways first. Then, as we grow in our discernment and our familiarity with His voice, our ability to tell when it really is His voice increases. Then, He calls us to follow Him a little further.

In the days after Sarah's healing, I was just starting down this road. My eyes had just been opened, and it was all new to me. I was learning how to discern, and I desperately wanted to hear the voice of God and to follow His lead. I knew He was speaking, but I wasn't confident in my ability to rightly hear Him or understand Him. I was learning to listen, and I had many language lessons still ahead.

During this time, a feeling was rising within me—a growing impression that we weren't to return to Central Asia. I immediately identified this as being from the devil, the enemy of our souls. It was so obviously contrary to what God had told us before. I felt it had to be an attack or a distraction, so I prayed against it. I put into practice the things we'd been learning about the spiritual world and stood my ground with the understanding that, because of the finished work of Christ, I could resist the Devil and he would have to flee from me. But it didn't work.

The feelings grew stronger, not weaker. I wondered if they might be a result of my own fears or misgivings about returning to the place where Sarah's illness had begun. I recruited Sarah to pray with me against these feelings. Sarah confided in me that she too had been feeling that we weren't supposed to return. We recruited friends to pray with us, but the more we prayed, the more clearly we understood that these feelings weren't from ourselves or from the enemy. They were from God.

We were confused by this at first, and we resisted. But as we sought His face and opened ourselves to His guidance, He confirmed this to our souls. We had experienced His power and His love. We knew He had good plans for us, but we couldn't understand why He wouldn't allow us to return to Central Asia. We loved it there, we had seen Him use us there and everyone expected us to return and rejoiced with us in that possibility. We found ourselves asking Him what He would have us do instead. He didn't answer immediately. I found waiting on Him to be much more difficult than doing things for Him. The waiting seemed to drag on and on, but in the end, we didn't have long to wait—a few weeks perhaps.

About a month after Sarah's healing, one of our supporting churches invited me to help them. We'd helped plant this church a few years earlier. It had started well but seemed to be wandering a bit. People were leaving the church. Most of the core was still there, but the leaders had a sense that something wasn't quite right. They asked me to help them figure out what was going on. I agreed to help them as a consultant.

Over the next couple of months, I met with many members and former members of the church. I listened and asked questions. Slowly, a picture emerged of divided leadership. There were competing visions for the direction of the community, and the leaders weren't pulling in the same direction. Instead, they were sharing their individual visions and disparaging the competing visions.

As the picture came into focus, I was concerned, not at all sure the leaders would like to hear what I'd found. This wasn't just an organization I was consulting with, this was my community. These leaders were my friends. I was going to have to walk into a meeting and tell them that the problem was in the room. They were the problem, and that's never a comfortable message to deliver.

I prayed a lot. I was looking for a way out, hoping God would let me off the hook. Instead, I felt a growing confidence that my diagnosis was accurate. I sought counsel from a few trusted friends and from Sarah. No matter which way I turned, I was faced with the same answer. I had to tell them.

The day of the meeting arrived, and I delivered the message to stunned silence. After a few minutes and a few cursory questions, I left them to their discussion. I had no idea what would happen, but I'd delivered the message I thought God had asked me to deliver. I would have to trust Him with the result.

The next day, I received a call from the pastor, who was a close personal friend. I'd been concerned about how the meeting would affect our relationship. He told me the associate pastor had resigned and the leadership had unanimously decided to invite me to come help fix the problems I'd identified.

I was shocked. I wasn't looking for a job. I was looking to get back overseas. I had spent the last couple of months looking at the dark underside of the church and had been commissioned to diagnose the problem, not to craft a solution. Frankly, I wasn't eager to wade into the mess. I talked about it with Sarah, and we took it to prayer.

Over the next few weeks, it became clear that this was to be our ministry. As I prayed, a vision for what needed to happen slowly emerged. I was only willing to make a one-year commitment, harboring the hope that this was a temporary detour and that we would return to Central Asia before long. I drew up a list of things that needed to happen, a plan for healing and change for the church. This plan also served as a list of conditions. If the leaders didn't agree that this was the right direction, then I would be off the hook.

At the top of the list was the resignation of the current leaders. I proposed that all the leaders spend a weekend away, searching the Scriptures and their own hearts about the call of leadership. At the beginning of the weekend, they would all resign. At the end of the weekend, we would mutually agree to a new slate of leaders. I thought this would be a deal-breaker.

Much to my surprise, the leaders agreed to all of my conditions. I was out of excuses again. I recognized this as God at work. The Father had clearly led me through the whole process by His Spirit, but this time, I was not being dragged along kicking and screaming. This time, I experienced the sweet gift of partnering and communicating with Him throughout the process. Rather than gritting my teeth and submitting, I was learning to enjoy the ride. I was learning to actually walk with God.

I spent the next year co-pastoring the church and helping it through a time of healing. We launched a prayer ministry and refocused the vision and the ministries. We saw new life birthed in the church, and it was a great year for us and for the church.

Toward the end of the year, I came across the list in the bottom of a drawer. My eyes scanned down the list, remembering how difficult it was to dream that big. In one incredible year, God had done it all. I could hardly believe what He had accomplished, amazed that He had invited me to do it with Him. And I could see that our work there was finished.

With eager anticipation, we began again to refocus our efforts on returning to Central Asia. With the blessings of the church, I took some time off to travel back to Central Asia to line up our visas and set things in motion for our return. The trip went well, and the doors to Asia were swinging open. We were eager to get back to that corner of the world. We'd left part of our hearts there, and we prayed that God would bless our plans to return.

But God had other plans.

CHAPTER 19

TWISTS AND TURNS

Just days after I got back from that trip to Central Asia, God began to lay another path before us. I met a man, Pete, who invited me to help him launch a new ministry based in the States that would identify and support effective ministries and projects in the Muslim world. He'd previously attempted to launch the organization without success and was looking for someone with field experience to help him. It sounded like a great idea, and I was happy to help him in my free time as I prepared to return to Central Asia.

Pete represented a small group of wealthy Christians who believed God had blessed them so they might be a blessing to the world. They believed they were responsible to be good stewards of the resources God had entrusted to them. They didn't want to just throw money around but wanted to invest it wisely in projects that would yield spiritual fruit.

Pete often referred to the vision as being "God's plumbers." There were pools of resources in the world, and there were places where these resources could do a lot of good. The problem was building the pipes to connect the resource reservoirs with the dry places. Pete's vision was to identify strategic and important projects around the world that needed resources and to mobilize prayer, people and money to meet these needs.

It was an exciting model. In my time overseas, I'd seen many unmet needs, and I'd also seen how money could damage and create dependency. I recognized the need for wisdom and discernment in this endeavor, and was excited for the vision to take shape and become reality. It wasn't difficult to see that God was at work in Pete and his friends.

Pete frequently asked me to consider staying in the States to lead the ministry, but I steadfastly and repeatedly refused. I was eager to return to Central Asia and was eager to continue investing in the lives of individuals—the type of ministry I'd so enjoyed. I was relieved when Pete stopped asking.

A few months later, he approached me again. We'd been working together and building a good relationship, and he said that he and the board had been praying a lot about this. They felt the Lord was confirming me as the right man for the job. As I began to turn him down yet again, he asked if I had prayed about it. That made me pause.

I had to confess I hadn't prayed about it at all. I protested that I didn't need to pray because I was sure we were supposed to go to Central Asia. He asked me to take some time to pray about it before answering, and I grudgingly agreed. The truth is I didn't want to pray about it because I didn't want to hear what God had to say afraid of any more twists and turns in the road. I wanted to return to Central Asia, but I also had other concerns.

I recognized that leading this kind of ministry would be radically different than what I had done before. I saw the need for it but didn't see myself in that kind of role. I was also afraid for my reputation. All of our friends and supporters expected us to return to Central Asia after Sarah's healing. Most had understood our decision to stay and help the church through a rough patch. Over the last few months, we'd been building momentum toward a return. What would it look like for me to switch directions now? All my friends and family, our pastors and counselors—the same ones who had urged us to come back from Central Asia—were now urging us to return.

One of my deepest concerns was for my own soul. The offered position would make me the counselor and confidant of people with great wealth. They would look to me for answers and input. I knew my own propensity for pride and was concerned that being in that role would only serve to feed my ego. I was afraid it might lead me away from God and the sweetness of dependence I'd been experiencing with Him. But how do you refuse to pray about something? I asked God what He would have me do and desperately hoped He wouldn't answer.

A few nights later, I awoke sometime after midnight to a strange sensation. It felt like someone was pressing on my head. My initial impression was that Sarah had shifted in her sleep and that her arm was lying across my head. As I reached up to move her arm, there was nothing there. I rubbed my head and turned over, but the pressure didn't disappear. I prayed against it, but it didn't go away. I tossed and turned hoping it would fade. I searched for a more comfortable position to be able to get back to sleep. After more than two hours of this, I relented and got out of bed. A suspicion had grown into a certainty: It was the Lord, and He wanted to have a talk with me.

I headed for the living room of our tiny apartment, hoping not to wake Sarah or our daughter. The pressure on the side of my head had continued and now solidified. It was almost as if someone was trying to insert a book into my head as you would insert a tape into a VCR. I decided to read some Scripture to clear my head and help me focus. I picked up the Bible and flipped it open to Paul's letter to the Galatians. I decided on Galatians because we'd been preaching through it at church, and I had a sermon coming up. I hadn't really expected to meet God in that book, but there in the middle of the night, God ambushed me in my own living room.

From the very first words of the book, God was speaking to my soul: "Paul, an apostle sent not from men nor by man, but by Jesus Christ and God the Father…" Those words were spoken to me so personally in that moment! I knew that God was speaking to me through them, reminding me that He sent me where He willed. I was not sent from men or by man. This spoke to my concern about what others would think.

As I read further, I found God speaking to me in section after section and confirming His call to me. He never said it would be easy. That night, through Galatians, He affirmed it would be hard. It would be dangerous for my soul, but He also said that through this, I would learn greater dependency on Him. He promised that He would be with me, that He was calling me to this and that He would take care of it all.

It was the most clear and direct communication I'd ever had from the Lord, up to that point in my life. It was amazing and reassuring! I still had reservations and was more than a little unclear on the details, but I was confident God had spoken to me. I knew He had good things in store, even though the path was going to be a difficult one.

It's odd that it was harder for me to hear His call to stay than it was for me to hear His call to go. I suppose the simple fact is that the call to go appealed to me, but the call to stay did not. A part of me enjoyed the adventure of the missionary life. Another part of me hungered for the acclaim of men. There is a small sense of celebrity that is afforded to missionaries in Christian circles, and sometimes missionaries start to believe what other people say about them. If I had a nickel for every time someone told me they admired me, or that they could "never do what you do," I would be a very wealthy man indeed. That can be heady stuff to a thirsty soul.

A friend of mine in Central Asia once said, "At least I'm better than all the Christians in America! At least I'm here, while they stayed home!" I was speechless. She had said aloud what others felt. It is so twisted, arrogant and wrong, but it's what sometimes happens in the heart of a missionary. We can begin to congratulate ourselves for our willingness to "leave it all." Perhaps we never actually left it at all; we've simply traded cisterns. We've chosen to give up the creature comforts of our home countries to enjoy the accolades and status that come with being a pastor or a missionary.

It was with some difficulty that I submitted to God's call to stay in the States. Over the next few weeks, our decision was met with dismay and some condemnation by our friends, both overseas and in the States. Many were sure that we had gotten soft, that we were taking the easy way out. Others questioned our commitment to the Lord or our ability to discern His will for our lives. It was a difficult time of transition.

We were blessed financially by the job and found it more difficult to be blessed than we'd imagined. We'd grown comfortable with little, but now had to learn how to honor God when we had much. The job paid well, but it was very difficult for me. I grew in many areas of administration and management that didn't come easily. There were many opportunities to restrain my pride as people I respected looked to me for guidance.

God blessed us in every way imaginable during that time. I had a good paying job, we bought a home and a couple of cars, and God blessed us with a son. We were living the American dream, and it was hard to resist the temptation to join the rat race. It was easy for us to sit in judgment from our perch overseas as we cast aspersions on those caught up in the busyness, shallowness and consumerism of American culture. Our vantage point was quite different when we were immersed in it. Each culture attempts to force us into ways of thinking, speaking and acting that are normal within the culture but often are directly in conflict with God's ways. I felt that tension in new ways during this season of my life.

During those years in America, we found ourselves drawn into a swirl of activity and consumption, and it was difficult for us to find time for our souls. My job paid well but required a lot of travel and could be quite stressful. We were also very involved in our local church and had a wide network of friends and family. It was a rich time as we learned a lot, gave a lot and received a lot. However, there were times when we felt we were running so fast our souls couldn't keep up.

We knew that we were doing what God wanted us to do. He didn't just set us on that path and disappear. He was with us all along the way. We saw some friends and family come to faith in Jesus. We saw the ministry with Pete blossom and bear fruit in the lives of the peoples of the Middle East, to the glory of God. I was continuing to learn how to collaborate with God and rely upon Him in ministry, and we were continuing to seek Him and to find Him working in and through our lives.

One day we received an email, out of the blue, from some old friends. Although we hadn't spent much time with Joe and Esther, we considered them friends. There are people you come across in life and think, "Wouldn't it be a dream come true if we could be in each other's lives!" That is how we felt about Joe and Esther. We'd never lived in the same place as they, but each time our paths crossed, we connected. They were writing to us now to invite us to join a new team they were putting together. They went so far as to lay out their vision for what I would do as a part of the team.

They'd been asked to assemble a team to lead, coach and care for missionaries across the Middle East and Asia. They knew East and Central Asia, but they were looking for someone with experience in the Middle East. They were looking for someone with a pastor's heart and leadership experience to come alongside them to live and work in community.

From the moment I read the letter, I couldn't stop smiling. The team and the position they described were a perfect fit, and I couldn't help but wonder if God might actually allow us to move back overseas. Could it be that we would get to work with these good friends? I printed out the message and handed it to Sarah.

She couldn't believe it. With Sarah's blessing, I sent it to some close friends and family members for their prayer and input. My mother's response stands out in my memory. She said that, as soon as she read it, she knew we were supposed to go overseas again and that she'd already started missing the grandkids.

Over the next few months, we talked with Joe and Esther several times as we sharpened the vision and worked on the details. We even traveled to visit a city in the Middle East as a potential site for the team. As we took these first tentative steps down this road, we felt the Lord's confirmation again and again.

We didn't want to launch out just because we wanted to, and we wanted to be careful to seek His direction. We'd learned that His plans for us are always good, and He had proven Himself time and time again. The Lord blessed every step we took. He brought the right buyer for our house, found a replacement for the ministry I'd been doing and led us through the process of assembling a prayer and financial support network. A little more than a year after our first conversation with Joe and Esther, we got on a plane and headed back overseas.

CHAPTER 20

LIFE IN COMMUNITY

We weren't headed back to our beloved Central Asia, but at least we were heading back overseas. This new assignment was different than our previous ones. Instead of working closely with local people, we would be working primarily with missionaries. We were joining a leadership team, and our role was to empower, equip and encourage missionaries. Our team was responsible to serve more than 200 adults and almost as many children, spread across eight time zones.

We decided to settle the team in a major city in the Middle East, which would keep us close to many of the workers. It would also allow us to experience the environment they worked in. Although our primary ministry was to the workers in our organization, that didn't prevent us from falling in love with our neighbors. We wanted to see them set free to experience the kind of life we'd found in union with the Father.

One of the great joys of this season was the team. As God knit our hearts together with this small group of people, they became much more than co-workers. They became family. We all lived in the same neighborhood of the sprawling metropolis. We had no office, but worked out of our homes, which meant we were constantly in and out of each other's space and deeply involved in each other's lives.

We were a diverse and multi-generational group, with members from various cultural and theological traditions and every age bracket and stage of life, from infancy through retirement age. All this diversity could have made for a difficult time; instead, it made for a rich stew of perspective and experience.

In the eyes, in the hearts and in the lives of these people, I saw the life of Jesus being lived out as wildly different people struggled through their differences. I saw aspects of the image of God in perspectives or personalities that I would have rejected out of hand before. I saw them struggle with crisis as they experienced tragedy, and I saw them wrestle for faith in the face of cancer. I didn't just observe. I experienced it with them, and I came to a startling realization on that team: Life in community is the heart of the gospel.

As an American, I was raised to value independence. Our country, and in many ways our culture, started with the Declaration of Independence, and we've never looked back. Individualism is the constant undercurrent, the assumed truth, behind the world I grew up in. It's the unquestioned assumption, and those are the most dangerous kinds of assumptions because they influence us from beneath the surface.

But what if an individual isn't meant to be a rock and an island? What if we were designed for community? What if, beneath it all, there wasn't an individual, but a community? What if community is the underpinning for all that exists? What if God is not an individual, but a community? The oft-overlooked truth is that this is the case. It always has been.

God is community, and He has always existed as a community: the Father, the Son and the Holy Spirit. Before the creation of light, before space and time and before life as we know it, there was community.

The good news is that God has invited us into this community life. According to Jesus' disciple Peter, when we embrace Christ we become "partakers of the divine nature." We get to participate in the eternal life of God. We don't become God. We don't replace God. We are welcomed into the family. We get to listen to their music, to join the dance they've been enjoying from eternity past. We get to be part of it all. We get a portion of this promise now, the deposit of the Holy Spirit, but we groan for the full revelation of the glory of God. We long for the full expression of the joyous riot that is the fellowship of the Trinity.

Community is at the core of God, and it should be at the core of our understanding and expression of the Kingdom of God and the family of God on earth. We've traded away this truth in our search for freedom and independence, and we've cut ourselves off from the joy of community. But it will not stay hidden. God is bigger than that.

I see now that part of my journey has been to uncover the treasures that have always been there. My heart was veiled, but these treasures have been available all along. Perhaps that's why Scripture is filled with references to those who have eyes but cannot see, ears but cannot hear.

As I lived and worked with my team, more of the scales fell from my eyes. We met weekly for prayer and worship. We carried the burdens of our friends scattered across Asia. We laughed together, played together and cried together. We even fought with each other. I had grown to place a high value on community. I knew it was important, but until this team, I hadn't experienced it to the same degree. There is a joy to be found in community that few ever find, and fewer still diligently seek.

Community requires risk. It's risky to love, to submit your will and your desires, to others. What if they are as selfish as I fear they will be? Community requires trust and faith, but it also requires humility. That was one of the hardest parts for me.

As you will no doubt have noticed by now, I have an almost unbelievable propensity for pride. Like a divine masseuse, God has consistently massaged this spot. He has pressed, prodded and stretched me to help work this knot out of the muscle of my soul. He has used the experiences of life and my own foolish choices. He has used community. He has also used the Scriptures.

Once, when reading Matthew 10, I found myself feeling bad for Thaddaeus. Almost all of the other disciples have a parenthetical comment after their names. Simon (also called Peter), Andrew (Peter's brother), Matthew (the tax collector), even Judas Iscariot (who later betrayed Him) got a line. But Thaddaeus is just Thaddaeus. I felt bad for him. As I reflected on this, I realized that I wasn't feeling bad for him. I was feeling bad for me. God gently probed my heart and showed me that my pity for Thaddaeus was actually a reflection of my own desire to be noticed and commented on.

Sometimes God wasn't so gentle. Once, I was attending a small gathering of leaders in Asia. We were all going out to dinner together, and everyone met in the lobby. When all were assembled, the group left—without me. I was deeply hurt, and my pain immediately flared into anger. How dare they forget *me!* God used His Word and experiences like this to continue the process of winnowing my soul. He reminded me of all the times in my life when I'd been forgotten and goaded me to recall that I was, apparently, imminently forgettable. At the same time, He assured me that He noticed me and loved me. He saw me and loved me as a perfect Father.

Humility is the unsung virtue. We don't generally desire humility, but in fact, humility is the doorway to freedom. Humility isn't seeing ourselves as nothing, looking down on or devaluing ourselves. True humility is to understand who we are and who we're not. Andrew Murray tells us that the ground of all humility is understanding that we are creatures, not the Creator. My father used to say it this way, "There is a God in heaven, and you are not Him!"

When we admit that we're not God, we've taken the first step toward right understanding. We're beginning to release the illusion of control, and we can relax a bit as we allow that to sink in. The earth will keep spinning without us. My mother is fond of saying that when you start feeling like you are indispensable, put your finger in a glass of water. Pull it out quickly and look at the hole you've left behind.

It's not that we're not important. It's that the ground of our importance isn't in what we do. We're important because we are image bearers, unique in all creation because we bear the image of God. In each of us there is a unique reflection of something of the character of God. The Father created us each on purpose. God knit us together and invested us with life and power, and we are all His children, wanted and loved. We are important because we are important to Him, magnificent creations from the Master Craftsman.

True humility allows me to recognize the beautiful parts of myself as well as the needy and dependent parts. We're flawed and often wrong about any number of things. Yet, we are beautiful. We were designed to be beautiful to show off the greatness of God. Marveling at God's workmanship isn't a bad thing. Though I must admit that marveling at His workmanship in myself is harder for me than recognizing it in others.

Recognizing what God put in me is also to recognize what I lack. I may be good with the big picture but lousy at details, great at being present in the moment but lose track of time far too easily. As I recognize the gifts, I can see the flip side as well. God has given me a portion of His image to show to the world. He hasn't invested a complete picture of Himself in any one person. We each have a portion of the image, but not all of it. We need other people.

Humility is the doorway to freedom and also to community. Humility trains me to see myself, as well as everyone else, through the eyes of God. It allows me to admit my limitations and to embrace the gifts of others. I can rejoice in the things that others can do better than I can. I can marvel at their gifts and let them shine without being threatened, succeed without feeling like a failure. I can be dependent on them.

We were designed to be dependent. We have needs. It's not bad. It's part of being a creature. We're dependent on food, water and air. We're dependent on people, and we're dependent on God. It's in our nature.

When we declare our independence, we cut ourselves off from the sweetness of community. We cut ourselves off from God, the sweetest community.

My life with my team helped me realize that God had been drawing me into His community from before I was born. At each stage in my journey, He's orchestrated events and relationships into an incredibly complex symphony of courtship. He's loved me with a Father's love before I even knew what that meant.

CHAPTER 21

THE FATHER'S HEART

Growing to understand the Father's heart has been a complex part of the journey for me. At various points along the way, He's placed men in my life to help me. On my team in the Middle East, He gave me the privilege of being in community with wonderful, strong, godly men. They've influenced me deeply, and I'm grateful for them.

Of course, my own father was the first and most influential man in my life. He wasn't perfect. He was a flawed man, as we all are. I've dwelt a lot on the difficult aspects of our relationship in this book, and many of the obstacles and issues I had to overcome can be traced back to his issues. I recognize that now.

An important part of moving forward in my relationship with my Father God was to make my peace with my earthly father. This was complicated by the fact that he died in the early stages my journey. I miss him. I wish I could have him read this book, and then talk about our journeys. I think he would be shocked and surprised—perhaps a bit hurt. Nevertheless, I think it would make him smile to see the way God has orchestrated the whole thing.

God brought this to light for me in the most unlikely way I can imagine.

During my years on the leadership team, I did a lot of traveling. Our people were scattered to the wind, and I often was flying out to meet with one or more of them. On a flight from somewhere to some place, God ambushed me. He spoke to me through a cartoon.

On this particular plane, each seat had a personal entertainment system. Each person could select any number of things to watch or listen to. It was a long flight, and I watched a movie or two. I slept for a while, and when I woke up, there wasn't enough time left on the flight to watch another movie.

I poked around for something shorter to watch. I came across a cartoon with the unlikely title of *God, the Devil and Bob*, an animated television series I'd never heard of it. The title alone demanded investigation, but little did I know that even in this God was pursuing me.

The general idea of the series is that God and the devil make a deal that the fate of the universe will hinge on a particular person, Bob, choosing between them. The episode I saw had to do with Bob and his father. Toward the end of the episode, Bob and God are sitting in a bar having a beer and talking. Bob is angry at his father and at God. God takes it all in and then shares His perspective on the situation.

The cartoon God tells Bob something like this: "Every father from Adam until today has punched his son. In every generation, my hope is that they will pass along a softer punch. Your grandfather really hammered your father. You're angry because your father punched you. I understand. Your father passed along a softer punch."

I sat in there in my seat weeping, just weeping. I thought about the way my father had failed me. I recognized that his failures were a result of his own woundedness. He was passing along the punches he had received. It didn't mean that he didn't hurt me, but it meant that I could view him through eyes of compassion. I could see him as a man and a peer rather than an icon in my memory.

Henri Nouwen, in his book *The Wounded Healer*, encourages us to view others in a similar way. He grounds our compassion in recognition of our own woundedness. Only a person who is aware of his own woundedness can be a source of healing for others. Our wounds are redeemed through their transformation into sources of compassion and healing for ourselves and for others. Nouwen encourages us to recognize that we view the actions of others through the lens of how they affect us. Then he encourages us to change that focus—to ask ourselves what would make them act that way, to push past their anger and recognize that it springs from a wound, just like our own anger does.

When we can do that, we can view them with real compassion, and we can offer them the compassion we have for ourselves. On that plane, watching that cartoon, God broke through to me. I was able to forgive my father and view him with compassion.

Another key way God has helped me to understand His heart as a father is through my own experiences as a father. Parenting has been an incredible part of my journey, as it has revealed aspects of my relationship with God that I couldn't have anticipated. By learning to love and serve my own children, I've begun to discover aspects of the Father heart of God that were previously veiled to me.

As I tuck my kids in at night, wrap them in my embrace or wipe away a tear, I am expressing the heart of God. I'm amazed that the God of the universe loves me even more than I love my own children. God—who spoke the universe into being—rejoices over me with singing and quiets me with His love. He is always watching me and always caring for me, working all things for my good.

I have to admit this hasn't always been my experience of Him. I've often wondered where He is and why He seems distant or silent. My own love for my children and my desire to protect them has caused me to wonder why God doesn't do a better job of protecting His children. Just a couple of years ago, I had a fresh realization of this in a moment of unguarded prayer.

I've discovered there are many levels to prayer and many kinds of prayer. Some of these use words while others don't. Even within worded prayer, there are a number of levels for me. Sometimes my prayers are familiar: themes and phrases I've previously prayed or experienced are recounted and re-prayed. Sometimes my prayers are carefully spoken and monitored for theological correctness or biblical soundness, even as they are forming on my tongue. But sometimes the words come unbidden.

These prayers spring up out of my soul and escape my lips before I have time to catch them. This is perhaps the deepest kind of worded prayer, as they express the unmonitored and unedited truth of our experience, bubbling up out of our souls. They can often sound harsh. They can say things to God that are unworthy of Him. Sometimes they are shouted, or quietly wept. Sometimes they are bitter. These are the authentic prayers of our souls, and as such, can be quite revealing.

I was in one of these deep times of worded prayer when I suddenly heard my voice say, "Please Lord protect my children! Please protect them better than you protected me!" I heard these words almost before I thought them. I stopped. They were hanging in the air. What had I just said? What had I just accused God of?! I felt an almost overwhelming need to explain away the bad theology embodied in those few words. *God hasn't failed to protect you,* I told myself. However, I remained unconvinced. I knew that my experience of God's failure to protect me from abuse was my real experience. It did no good to let Him off the hook with theological arguments. It was time that I hash this out with God.

I love that God is big enough to handle my emotions, secure enough not to be threatened by honest questions. He may not answer them, but I think He loves it when we're bold enough to ask them. The book of Job in the Old Testament teaches us this.

So began a deep and difficult period in my relationship with the Father. I wanted to know where He'd been when I was being abused. My friends assured me He was there and shared their experiences of Him, but those were their experiences, not mine. I knew if I saw someone preparing to abuse my children as I had been abused, I would do anything and everything in my power to stop it. I knew that God wasn't short on knowledge, foresight or power. Yet He had done nothing to prevent my abuse. Could I trust a God who promised to defend His children and then failed to do so?

I struggled with this question for months. I continued to work and live as before. I shared the struggle with my team, and they prayed for me. But this was something I had to wrestle with on my own. I felt like Job, trying to lay hold of God and force him to answer my question, or like Jacob grasping at God and refusing to let go until He blessed me. Again, I was at a moment of crisis in my faith. As this dark night of the soul dragged on, I didn't feel that God was distant as much as beckoning me onward. This is an excerpt from my journal at that time:

I believe it is the Lord beckoning me to return to the depths of my soul. These are the deep places, the oft dark places, the places from which my motivations and desires spring. These are the places that go unexamined most of the time, and that is not a bad thing in and of itself. To visit these wild regions of the heart is a perilous and consuming thing. You could not live in this place forever, but to reject the invitation to this part of the journey would be to reject the invitation to growth, to healing. It would be to reject the invitation of God.

Accepting this invitation is like entering a deep gorge. At first there is some excitement as you marvel at the view. The vista is grand, and the scenery interesting. The sense of adventure is almost palpable. The canyon gapes before you, you see the path winding downward and you can hardly wait for the adventure to begin. As you follow the path downward, the walls grow ever higher on either side of you. Their immensity is awe inspiring. The shadows start to grow deeper and fall ominously across your path. As you move deeper into the defile, you start to grow somewhat apprehensive.

What will be around the next bend? Where is this road leading you? You start to slow down. The path feels familiar under your feet. It is as if you have been here before, but it is not a comfortable kind of familiarity. It is simultaneously familiar and frightening. You start to feel anxious. The hair stands up on the back of your neck. The canyon walls are no longer beautiful or interesting to your eyes. They now seem more menacing as they tower over you. They seem to close in on you as you move ever onward, ever downward. You start to feel like turning back. Now the canyon is so dark that you are really afraid. You can't see the way forward clearly, but you are beckoned onward. The walls are so close now that you are bumped and bruised. You remember this feeling. You remember this fear. This is what you ran from years ago. This is what you spent so many years avoiding. These are the feelings you have been denying and protecting yourself from for so long.

Now the canyon has narrowed so far that you have to turn sideways and push yourself through the crevice before you. The only way forward will be painful, but to turn back is unthinkable. You have come this far. He beckons you on. He assures you it will be all right. But can you trust Him? He has allowed you to be hurt before. Can you trust Him?! Where else can you go? Who else has the words of eternal life? And so, you plunge yourself in the crevice, getting scraped and scratched, battered and bloodied, trusting that He will not mislead you, that He has not lead you here to abandon you. You cannot see where He is leading, but you choose to trust.

As you struggle on, fear grips your heart. You have been down here a long time. You are not sure how much more of this you can take. You start to doubt. What if you were wrong? What if you have deceived yourself, and He didn't really ask you to take on this journey? After all, it doesn't seem like anyone else is taking a journey like this. Why do you have to do this while others seem to do just fine without having to endure the darkness, this dark night of the soul?

This went on for several months. I desperately wanted to be out of the valley, but I couldn't reason my way out. I couldn't theologize or think my way out. I needed God to meet me there. I knew He was there but always tantalizingly out of reach.

All during this time, I was searching for God, reading His Word and praying. I was worshiping and fellowshipping with His people. I was frequenting all the places where we'd met in the past. I was seeking to understand His Father heart for me and why my good and powerful Father had failed me, asking Him to explain to me where He was in my abuse. He refused to answer but kept drawing me deeper into the pain, and I wondered if He was going to drag me under for good. Then, one day, God ambushed me at church.

We were late for some reason, and the only seats left were in the front row. We took our seats just as the worship was beginning. We were singing "How Deep the Father's Love for Us" by Stuart Townend. I didn't feel anything in particular until we sang these words: "The Father turns His face away, as wounds which mar the chosen One bring many sons to glory." I was suddenly overcome with emotion. I began weeping in the front row of the church. I don't know how to describe what happened in that moment. I can only say that God touched me in a very personal way. I still struggle to understand it entirely or to explain it clearly.

It wasn't a verbal experience. God didn't say anything specific as much as I suddenly understood things differently and knew that He was there as the wounds that marred me were inflicted. He was there, but He chose to turn His face away in that moment as I would turn my face away if I couldn't bear to watch something terrible happening. I also had incredible assurance that these wounds were inflicted to bring many sons and daughters to glory.

He had allowed it on purpose as a part of His greater plan. He too had suffered as one of His children suffered through the abuse. He didn't fail to protect me; it was all part of His plan. In the days that followed, He brought to mind many people I was able to help with their own difficult recovery from abuse. I could help them because of what I had suffered.

My suffering is a part of the good plan that He is working out. It isn't redemptive in the same way the sufferings of Christ are, but it does play a part in the larger story of redemption. I am now uniquely positioned to comfort others with the comfort I have received.

I recognize that this message won't resonate with everyone. I share the specifics not to provide another principle to be applied—or rather misapplied—when others are suffering. I share it to illustrate the necessity of responding to and interacting with God in the midst of our pain. Many of my friends tried to help me during this dark period. They wanted it to be over, so they tried to show me shortcuts out of the valley. But God wanted me to go into and through the valley to provide another level of healing, another level of relief, another level of understanding, a deeper kind of intimacy.

I believe we often miss opportunities for intimacy with God because we want to avoid the painful path. We would prefer to live comfortably in this world, even if it means missing the chance to be connected with the God of the universe. In doing so, I'm afraid we sometimes short circuit the growth of others by offering them platitudes, truths we would like them to grasp, because their pain makes us uncomfortable.

We don't want to see them suffer, but perhaps it's because we haven't plumbed those unfamiliar depths ourselves. Whatever the reason, the one needful thing is for us to sit at the feet of Jesus and to hear from Him. We must allow God to speak what He would have them learn in His time.

My journey into fatherhood has frequently called me to wrestle with the Father heart of God. I'm still mystified that God would love me, and I see all my foibles and failures so clearly in the light of Jesus' example. Then, I ponder the way I love my kids. I don't love them less when they make a mistake. I don't want them to earn their way back into my love. I love them because they are my kids. God loves me even better than I love them, and He isn't finished with me yet. He keeps shaping me, leading me and speaking to me.

CHAPTER 22

AN UNEXPECTED WORD

As I was emerging from this dark night of the soul, I went on a spiritual retreat that would change my life in most unexpected ways. Over the years, I've taken occasional spiritual retreats and have found them to be an incredible aid in my relationship with God. During my time on the team in the Middle East, Sarah and I regularly scheduled them as part of our routine.

I'd been introduced to silence and solitude years before, but only in the sprawling urban mass of that noisy Middle Eastern city did I start to practice it. There, in the community of my team, I pursued the Lord in silence and solitude.

For me, a retreat means disappearing for a day or more with only my Bible and a journal. Activity and accomplishment have always come more naturally for me than stillness. But in the stillness of a spiritual retreat, I've often heard my heart more clearly and, more importantly, have been able to hear God more clearly.

A spiritual retreat can take many forms. The point is to take time out to stop and to listen—time away from the normal activities of life. Our hearts are like a pool in a forest glade. The activities of our life swirl the water, and we fill our lives with noise and activity, stomping around in the pool until it is a murky mess. Suddenly, we drop our keys or something else important in the pool. We can thrash around in the water, urgently searching for what we've lost. But there is another option.

We can sit by the side of the pool and wait. The waiting is a choice, an action. As we wait, the silt settles, the water clears and we can see into the depths with greater clarity and grasp what we have been looking for.

This particular retreat was held in the quietness of my bedroom. Our home has never been a quiet one. I grew up in a noisy home, full of life and activity, and our home is like that. It's tough to find solitude and silence in that context, but I've discovered an invaluable aid in noise-cancelling headphones and calm music. I have an album specifically written to aid in contemplation and devotion. With the aid of these tools and a little concentration, I find I can carry my silence with me into almost any space where I will not be interrupted.

As I lay on my bed that afternoon, I was praying aloud to God. It isn't uncommon for me to spend some of my retreat time arguing with God, hashing things out with Him. When I do that, I often find it helpful to pray aloud even when I'm alone. Somehow praying aloud seems to crystallize my thoughts. I was just on the tail end of what had been a very difficult period and was glad to be out of it, but I still wondered what it had been about. I was laying my questions out before Him. Why had He put me through that? What was the purpose behind it? How was He going to redeem it? Where was He taking me next?

Just after I asked the last question, I heard a voice in the room. Not a whisper, a normal conversational tone. I heard a single word. I was startled by the interruption of my monologue, and immediately looked up to see who had intruded on my temporary sanctuary. There was no one there, so I got up and opened the door to see if one of the kids had strayed down the hall. No one was there. I opened the window and looked around to see if there was someone nearby. No one was there.

So, I attended to the unexpected word I had heard: "Wales." I knew the word I'd heard was the name of the small European country. It was Wales, not whales. I recalled that the word had been spoken after I'd asked God where he was taking me next, but I certainly hadn't expected a verbal response. In fact, I hadn't been asking a geographical question at all. I'd been asking a question about the nature of our relationship, and where our relationship was headed. Nevertheless, I was left with the name of this country, Wales, stuck in my head. I checked my memory: Had I recently read a book about Wales? Had I seen a movie? Had I read an article? Had the word arisen from my own subconscious? I asked the Lord, "Was that really you?" I waited … nothing. No response, no further word came.

Over the previous decade or so, I'd become more familiar with the voice of God. Through His Word, I had come to know His tone of voice and His character, as well as the content of His general will. I'd also had a variety of experiences through which I'd been learning to discern His communication to me specifically. Sometimes He spoke through other people, sometimes through music, often through the Scriptures. But never before had He spoken through an audible word.

I didn't know what to do with it, so I wrote it in my journal and treasured it my heart. I didn't tell anyone else, even Sarah. I simply didn't trust it. I didn't understand it. Even if it was God speaking, that only opened a larger mystery. We were happy where we were. We had a great team and a great ministry. We'd lived in this place longer than any other place in our entire married lives. It was our home, the only home my son could even remember. We had no connection with Wales. We had no reason to go there or any interest in moving at all. It wasn't even the question I asked!

Isn't it funny that God answers questions we never asked? I think about how Jesus responded to the woman at the well. She asked for a drink, and He told her to call her non-existent husband. Talk about a leap! Jesus seemed to specialize in puzzling questions and answers. I wonder if He doesn't do this to get our attention—to jar us out of our familiar ways of thinking. It certainly did that for me in this case.

Over the next couple of weeks, as I puzzled over the significance of the word, strange things started happening. Wales came up no fewer than eight separate and isolated times. I don't know if I'd ever had a conversation about Wales before. I was only dimly aware it even existed. It had never come up before, but now it was everywhere.

I was approached once by a complete stranger and asked if I was Welsh. That had certainly never happened before! I'd asked the Lord to confirm if the word had been from Him, and I was getting the distinct impression it was. I still didn't know why He had spoken it. I didn't know what its significance was to me. Somewhere in the middle of this time, I'd shared the odd phenomena with Sarah. She too was puzzled and wondering what God was up to.

For several months, Sarah had talked about a vague sense that God was going to do something new. She didn't have any more detail than that. In the coming weeks, God began to unveil different aspects of His plans for us. He started to move in my heart and in Sarah's about a new thing. He seemed to be birthing in us a deep desire for something new, but it was just out of reach. We felt as if we'd just catch a glimpse of it out of the corner of our eye, but when we turned to examine it, it would vanish. Then one day, it was staring us full in the face.

One Sunday evening, after we had put the kids to bed, we were sitting on the couch in our living room discussing the day. The conversation drifted to what God was teaching us. As we shared our hearts with one another, a vision started to materialize. In a matter of minutes, we had tremendous clarity on what we were supposed to do next. In just a few minutes, we'd jotted down notes that would guide us into the next stage of our journey with Him.

In the book of Acts, chapter six, we find a story about the apostles. They were doing a lot of good work, but they knew God was calling them to focus on "prayer and the ministry of the Word." As a result, they chose not to do other things. We felt like God was calling us in a similar way. We knew three things He was calling us to: simplicity, prayer and teaching.

Simplicity was about our lifestyle as well as our work. Where our work was concerned, it meant we were supposed to go deeper, not wider, working with only a few people and fewer projects. As we reflected on this, it became clear that He was asking us to step away from organizational leadership.

Prayer had been a growing part of our lives for the last few years, but we felt a keener sense of focus on this. Simplicity of work and lifestyle were linked to freeing up time for prayer. We'd grown to believe that prayer isn't just a support to the work of God. Prayer is work, a real and tangible thing we can do to affect the lives of people and nations. Whatever was next, prayer was a big part of it.

Teaching had been a part of our lives for many years. Both Sarah and I had opportunities to speak to groups of people, but we felt that God was asking us to take a different direction with our teaching. He seemed to be calling us to focus on life mentoring more than public speaking. There was also a new strain—a focus on writing.

Unfortunately, this vision meant we would need to leave our current role and team, something we were loath to do. We paused to pray about it, and as we did, we were overwhelmed with God's goodness and a strong sense we were supposed to move forward on this. We were still unclear on how the word I had received related to this change, but we knew it was time to tell the team.

The next morning I was scheduled to meet with the men from our team to hear from each other's hearts and pray for each other. The meeting started somewhat awkwardly, with both Joe and me saying we had big news to share with the team. After we did our best Chip and Dale routine, each trying to defer to the other, Joe started.

He shared that the previous evening God had given Esther and him great clarity about their future. They would be disbanding the team and moving in an entirely new direction. I then shared that Sarah and I had a similar experience the night before, and that we would be moving in a new direction as well. We stared at each other, trying to get our heads and hearts around what was happening.

God had brought us all together. We had tasted the sweetness of real community as we lived and worked together for six years. We had grown to love each other deeply. Now, it seemed that God was scattering us. It was a bittersweet time.

It was extremely hard to think about parting. God had knit our hearts together, and now they would have to be separated. No one was looking forward to that experience.

On the other hand, God was clearly at work. In His kindness, He spoke to both couples independently of the other, and He did it on the same night. It was amazing, and it was the first of many sweet confirmations that gave us confidence that the Father was orchestrating everything, working all things together for good.

CHAPTER 23

A TREASURE HUNT

The first steps toward leaving the team involved the team. We received the vision within the context of community, and we immediately requested their help. We gathered the whole team together and presented our hopes and aspirations, sharing how it had come about. We didn't share the word about Wales, because we weren't clear about how it related to what was unfolding. We also didn't want to bias their advice by pushing them toward a particular outcome.

We'd grown to appreciate the unique gifts of each of our teammates, and we wanted to hear their perspectives on what was happening. We weren't disappointed. They asked questions and probed in their areas of expertise, and as a result, we ended up with greater clarity about what we were supposed to do and how to do it.

In our previous roles, we had responsibility for specific geographic areas. To a large degree, this determined where we would base our team or, at least, it narrowed the options. Our new ministry wasn't tied specifically to geography. We could base it anywhere in the world.

Our team asked insightful questions to help us hone the vision and helped us come up with criteria for selecting a location. We ended up with a list of ten major criteria. Armed with this list, we began our research.

I didn't research Wales, hoping we would be in Asia. Most of our organization's workers were in that part of the world, and as word of the changes to our team started to get out, several of my friends in Asia pitched various locations for us to consider. Some of them seemed to fit the criteria fairly well.

Asia was familiar. It was the only part of the world I'd ever lived in, outside of the U.S. We had never even visited the U.K., other than flying through the airports on our way to somewhere else. That was soon to change.

I was due to attend a gathering of leaders from our organization in a few weeks. It turned out that this gathering would be in the U.K. I boarded the plane for the conference, feeling a little frazzled. In the midst of all that was going on, I hadn't finished my preparations for the meetings.

I settled into my seat, plugged in my headphones and tuned into the classical station on the flight. Before the plane even left the ground, I was off in another world, doing my homework. Suddenly, I heard a voice say, "Are you thinking about relocating internationally?" I smiled and thought to myself, "Yes, I am actually!" Then the voice said, "You should consider Wales."

I froze. I looked around to see if anyone else was hearing this! I glanced up and saw that British Airlines was running a public announcement. It was prefaced by a brief commercial for Wales. It wasn't quite miraculous, but it did get my attention. At the end of the commercial, I jotted down the website in the margin of my work paper. I decided I would look it up when I got a chance.

God was definitely at work, and He was speaking to us. We had clarity on the vision, and we were researching locations. However, we didn't have any idea how this new ministry would fit within our organization. It was definitely outside the mainstream of what our group focused on, but we were confident God was calling us to do it. However, we didn't know if that meant we'd need to leave the organization.

During that week in the U.K., I had the opportunity to talk about the vision with key leaders. Some encouraged me to run with it, while others were concerned that it was too far outside the box. By the end of the week, we'd received the endorsement of some key leaders and were strongly encouraged to run with it.

I called Sarah from the U.K. and shared the good news with her. We'd been willing to follow God, even if it meant leaving the community we'd found within our organization. It now appeared we wouldn't have to do that. We were relieved and eager to see how God would lead us into the future He was unfolding.

That week, I also checked out the Web site from the commercial on the plane. I researched all about Wales, and found that it perfectly matched all of our criteria. During that search, I also came across a little town in Wales that grabbed my attention. I suppose it was the history of the place that first drew me. I was still a historian at heart, and I decided that if we ever got that far, I wanted to check out that little town. I don't think I could reproduce the series of clicks to get onto the site for that little town. I've tried it. I don't know how I ended up there, but I knew I needed to check out the town.

I returned from that trip with a sense that we were off to the races. With the green light from the leaders, I felt free to run forward. We made plans for a trip to Wales, to see the country before we planned to move there. We made plans to leave our beloved team and to spend a few months in the States before moving to our new location. However, all of these plans came to a skidding and messy halt a few weeks later.

While we were initially encouraged to run with the vision, the story quickly changed. We were going through the channels to get official approval when our hopes were suddenly dashed, and it appeared that leaders who had once encouraged us privately refused to support us publicly. It was a confusing and frustrating time, and I felt betrayed by leadership once again.

Another challenge arose as more people started speaking into the process. It seemed everyone had their own ideas about what we should do. Our vision was batted around and began to morph before our eyes, our original goals getting lost in the shuffle. Our dream was being hijacked, as competing hopes and expectations from a diverse set of organizational leaders were imposed upon it. Eventually, that complex and confused vision collapsed as well. It couldn't bear up beneath the weight of expectation and the territorial politics within the organization.

The organizational politics aren't the point of the story, but they do illustrate the confusing ways God moves. Many people seem to think that when God is doing something, it will always go smoothly. If I've learned anything, I've learned that encountering difficulty doesn't mean God isn't at work. He uses difficulty, allowing the stones in the road—and sometimes tossing in a few Himself.

This confused and confusing process was also part of His plan. God was at work in all of it. He wasn't sleeping when these things were happening. His will wasn't being missed or thwarted. He was working out the timing, providing another opportunity for me to learn to trust Him.

In my experience, the journey is at least as important as the destination. We were learning to wait on Him, rather than rush ahead as I am so prone to do. We were learning to discern His voice from the voices around us. In hindsight, I think the process of learning to listen to Him was a key part of what He was doing in our lives at that time. It was part of His training for the next season of life.

Throughout this process, we were growing increasingly confident in our trajectory. We knew we were moving in the direction God wanted. Nevertheless, we didn't know how He was going to work it all out. It now appeared we would have to leave the organization after all. This was a big change of plans and would cause significant delays.

We were desperate for God to speak to us during this time. We were hearing His voice frequently, though not audibly. Nor was He answering the questions we were asking. He was guiding us as we ministered to people, and He was pressing on personal areas in our hearts. He just wasn't speaking to us about the specifics of location or any of the organizational questions. He wasn't telling us how to move forward with the vision He had birthed in us.

I imagine we were feeling something similar to Abraham. He heard the voice of God telling him to leave the land of his fathers—that much was clear. But God didn't tell him where he was headed, or how to get there. Abram had to launch out into the unknown. We were doing the same.

We were convinced about what God wanted us to do, and we were confident He would unfold the specifics in His time. In the meantime, we were left in a kind of no-man's land. We had left our team, put our things in storage and returned to the States to visit our family, all with the expectation that we would be moving to a new location within a few weeks or months.

We waited for the approval to come through. When that failed to materialize, we found ourselves back in the States with a dream but no way to bring it to fruition. One thing felt certain: We would never be able to move the vision forward within our current organization.

We remained in the States for a year. It was a year of ambiguity, as we made many false starts and received confusing signals. Then one day, I received a call from a leader in our organization. Our original proposal had been approved, and we were given the freedom to start a new team and to experiment with our new vision. We were also given permission to locate the team in Wales.

We didn't know who would be joining us. We were committed to ministry in community, and we had experienced the sweetness of a wonderful team life over the last few years. We'd originally hoped God would draw our old team along with us, but over that year, He scattered our cherished community to the ends of the earth.

We were initially disappointed; however, we had no doubt that He would provide. We wanted a team, but we didn't want to build a team in our own strength or rely on our own wisdom.

God brought many people to mind, but we were hesitant to approach them. We knew they were each involved in important work in their own corners of the world. In addition, the leaders in the various corners didn't seem keen to have us poaching good people from their areas. Eventually we were given permission to contact a family who had been on our hearts from the beginning.

They were friends from Central Asia, but not people we'd previously worked with. We'd known them for years and felt that their hearts and ours would align. We also knew their gifts would complement ours. On top of all of this, we really liked them. I wrote to them to share the vision and invited them to pray about joining us.

As only God could orchestrate it, they too had a sense God was leading them into something new—they had no idea what. They wanted to hear from Him alone, and not beat the bushes for opportunities. One morning in particular, they were crying out to God, asking Him to drop something specific right in their laps. A few minutes later, when they checked their email, the note from me had arrived. It briefly presented the vision and invited them to join us on the journey into the unknown. Just a few weeks later, we'd arranged to meet them in Wales.

We planned to scout out several potential locations. We had a number of towns on our list, but we decided to start with the one I'd found in my original Web search. We never even visited the others. Over the course of that visit, the Lord confirmed He'd gone before us and had selected this particular town for us. We had a sense that God had invited us to join Him on a treasure hunt, and He had hidden treasures for us all along the way: a historical detail, a word spoken over us, discovering a vibrant local church, a surprisingly deep connection with the pastor and his wife. Our task each day was to wait expectantly upon Him and then to follow the clues to discover what He'd placed there for us to find.

We found so many treasures that we sometimes stayed up late in the evening, marveling at the adventures of the day. There were appointments missed, but unexpected connections made. We had multiple flat tires and lost our way on the country roads more than once. It was slow going at first—not without trials or troubles. But through it all, it was clear that God was working behind the scenes, as over the course of the week, we developed a sense that God wasn't making a way for us as much as He was inviting us into something He was doing, a work in progress.

Perhaps the most amazing illustration of this was the house God had in store for us. One evening, about halfway through our trip, Sarah looked at me seriously and said she needed to tell me something, just to say it aloud. She said she could be wrong, but she thought God had just told her He was going to give us a house through a couple from the church. She told me they were going to rent it to us for a specific amount.

None of it made much sense at the moment, but we'd been on a treasure hunt and perhaps this was another clue to follow. The really troubling aspect for me was the amount. The number she mentioned was one-third to one-half of the rental value of houses in the town. I laughed and said I thought it all might work out, except for the price.

The following day, we met with the pastor of the local church. Unexpectedly, he mentioned that he knew a couple in the church who might have a house to rent. My ears perked up. Then he mentioned that they were out of town, and that he wasn't sure when they were returning. *False alarm,* I thought, but the next day the pastor called us and said the couple was back. They wanted to talk with us.

I called the number he gave me, and we talked by phone. They arranged to leave the house keys with their parents so we could have a walk through while they were at work the next day. We were amazed that this couple, whom we'd never met, would let us ramble through their house unattended. The following day, we fell in love with their house. It had a few architectural oddities, but we loved it.

The next evening, the night before we were returning to the States, the couple invited us to come for dinner. We had a wonderful time, sharing our stories and our journeys with God late into the evening. We found we were kindred spirits and that they were part of a network of truly amazing and vibrant believers in the town. Although we'd never previously met, we shared openly and talked deeply. As the evening was drawing to a close, we talked about the house.

They told us that God hadn't allowed them to sell the house for the last two years. About a year ago, He'd told them He was bringing a family to live in the house. They were confident we were that family. They asked if we knew the rental values for similar houses in town. We told them what the asking price would likely be, knowing we couldn't afford that much. They responded that they had a specific rent amount they felt was right. They named the exact number Sarah had mentioned three days previously. I nearly spilled my tea.

In this detail and a myriad of other ways, God led us not only to a town, but to a specific house. He provided a new team, new friends and companions for the journey from among our new neighbors. We know we are exactly where we need to be, exactly where He wants us. We know He is our God and He is leading us on this journey.

More importantly, He continues to journey with us. God has been pursuing me from before I was born. He knit me together in my mother's womb. He placed me in my family, in my country, in my culture. He did it all on purpose, so that I might turn to Him. He has pursued this thirsty fool through the journey of my life, and now I am pursuing Him too.

REFLECTIONS OF A THIRSTY FOOL

If the story seems to break off too abruptly, it's because it isn't over. The story of my life is only half written. I don't know how many chapters remain, but I do know there is still much to learn. I've only scratched the surface of the depths of God.

As I reflect back over the paths taken thus far, I see that this story isn't really about me. I'm not the protagonist, although I am the storyteller. The hero of the story of my life is the Triune God, Father, Son and Spirit. He's the one who has been pulling me forward, and carrying me along into the adventure He had planned for me before the foundation of the world.

It's an amazing adventure, and it is so much better when I choose to trust Him, when I don't leave His love unrequited. When I answer His pursuit of me, I find what I've been looking for—the peace and love we all know we've lost. For years, I didn't know where to find it. It was hidden in plain sight. Now, I run to Him. I'm answering His pursuit of me with a pursuit of my own. I'm still thirsty, but I hope a little less foolish.

I look back with wonder at how far He's carried me. In the beginning, he was dragging me, kicking and screaming, toward the Kingdom. To quote C.S. Lewis, I was "like a child making mud pies in a slum because I could not imagine a holiday at the beach." I was far too easily satisfied with lovers less wild. But the Lover of my soul came after me. He wasn't satisfied on my behalf. He knew that I would love being loved by Him.

Someone once told me that a wise man learns from his own mistakes, but that a truly wise man learns from the mistakes of others. In reading my story, you will have discovered that I'm not truly wise. I've made more than my share of mistakes along the way. It seems I have a tendency to learn things the hard way.

My hope is that you might learn from my mistakes. I hope you might be truly wise, that you will look through the rough and raw story of my life to see the One behind it. Through the chaos, you might hear the quiet strains of a masterpiece drifting through. There is beauty among the ashes. There is a work of art to be traced among the scars.

I pray that, as you read my story, you will be encouraged to reflect on your own. I don't know your story. I don't know your joy or your pain. I do know that God has met me in my pain, even though He didn't prevent it. I know He can do the same for you. I know He loves you. The final chapter of your story hasn't been written, but I'm sure that God's fingerprints are all over your life. He is already at work, and He has been wooing you from before the world was born.

I pray you will find some hope in my story, that you will find hope to really live, to reach out, to question, to probe. I hope you will be encouraged not to settle for less than all that God has for you. I pray you will search, you will seek, you will ask. For everyone who asks receives. He who seeks finds; and to him who knocks, the door will be opened.

The New Testament author John tells us that Jesus stands at the door and knocks. If anyone will listen for His voice and will respond by opening the door, He will come in and sit down to share a meal with you. You will know His fellowship for the journey. That has certainly been my experience.

My hope is that you will keep on asking, keep on seeking, and not give up. G.K. Chesterton once wrote, "The Christian ideal has not been tried and found wanting; it has been found difficult and left untried." Don't be afraid. The choice to pursue Him is a choice of reckless followership. It requires what Brennan Manning calls a "ruthless trust." We must press on in the face of uncertainty and unknowing, when the light seems to have faded into darkness. We must press on and never stop the pursuit.

I've seen far too many of my friends and companions on the journey give up. Some came to a difficult point and turned back, unwilling to risk the next passage. Some came to a comfortable place and set up camp, confusing a temporary resting place for the summit. Some struggled on alone, but eventually lost heart for the want of companions and dropped beneath their load. Some have simply become lost along the way.

To these I say, "Come with me! Don't give up! It's worth it! I haven't reached the destination, but I tell you there is joy in the journey! Come join those journeying toward God. You don't need to have all the answers, just the courage to ask honest questions. Among those searching you will find community. Don't rest until you've found at least one other soul with whom you can share the journey. There are more of us than you might think."

But there are others. Some have wrecked their lives by clinging to their own pain, as a twisted badge of honor. They've refused to let the

Healer touch their lives and relieve their burden. Some have hidden their hearts away and have lost themselves in their effort to avoid God. Some have turned to the cisterns and vainly seek to quench their thirst where there is no water. They mock those who continue to hope for, and search for, the fountain of living water. They're not content to wander off the path alone; they recruit others into their futile pursuit. They're not happy to ruin just their own lives; misery loves company. They heap abuse on those struggling on the journey, ridiculing them and making their journey ever more arduous.

To these I would say, "Hope again! It doesn't have to be this way! As you are, so once was I. You are welcome to come and journey with us! Come! Join us in our thirsty quest!"

Pioneers mobilizes teams to initiate church-planting movements among unreached peoples in partnership with local churches.

To get involved, visit Pioneers.org

To shop for more BottomLine titles—as well as other missions resources—visit Pioneers.org/Store